Dangerous Crooked Scoundrels

*Insulting the President, from
Washington to Trump*

EDWIN L. BATTISTELLA

OXFORD
UNIVERSITY PRESS

OXFORD
UNIVERSITY PRESS

Oxford University Press is a department of the University of Oxford. It furthers
the University's objective of excellence in research, scholarship, and education
by publishing worldwide. Oxford is a registered trade mark of Oxford University
Press in the UK and certain other countries.

Published in the United States of America by Oxford University Press
198 Madison Avenue, New York, NY 10016, United States of America.

© Oxford University Press 2020

CIP data is on file at the Library of Congress
ISBN 978-0-19-005090-0

1 3 5 7 9 8 6 4 2

Printed by Sheridan Books, Inc., United States of America

Contents

ONE

Insults and Politics

When I was growing up, trading insults was part of making your way through middle school: "If they put your brain on the edge of a razor blade, it would look like a BB rolling down a four-lane highway." "His parents had to put a pork chop around his neck to get the dog to play with him." "If you could teach him to stand still, you could use him for a doorstop." It was word-play, imagery, and linguistic sparring—a show for an adolescent audience.

Later, I learned about Shakespearean insults ("Thy tongue outvenoms all the worms of Nile"), along with those of Winston Churchill (said to have described his Labour Party rival Clement Atlee as "a modest man, who has much to be modest about"). I also learned about Oscar Wilde (who said of Henry James that he "writes fiction as if it were a painful duty") and Dorothy Parker (who described the novice actress Katharine Hepburn, appearing in *The Lake*, as running "the gamut of emotions from A to B").

I learned about the Celtic and Germanic traditions of flyting, which involve ritualized insult. In the Norse *Lokasenna* (*Loki's Wrangling*), the god of mischief trades insults with the other gods one by one. Loki tells Bragi, the god of poetry, "In thy seat art thou bold, not so are thy deeds, Bragi, adorner of benches!" Flyting was a stylized battle of wits, what we might think of as a medieval rap battle. Contemporary hip-hop treats us to similar lyrics, such as Lupe Fiasco's "I'm flying on Pegasus, you flying on a pheasant," and many more.

Wit and aesthetics can be part of an insult, but that is not always the case. An insult is ultimately an attack. The word itself, by way of French, is related to the Latin verb *insultāre*, meaning "to leap upon." In its earliest English occurrences in the sixteenth century, *insult* meant scornful boasting—what today we might call trash talking. By the early seventeenth century, the word was used in the modern sense: to assail another with contempt.

As the seventeenth century gave way to the eighteenth and the thirteen North American colonies became the new United States of America, political rivals employed insults with abandon. The practice has never ceased, and this book surveys more than five hundred presidential insults from the span of US history, painting a picture of the ways in which our chief executives have been verbally attacked in their times, how they have responded, and what we can learn from it all. Today's political scene may seem to be an age of unfettered hostility, with insults regularly flying at—and most recently from—the occupant of the White House. We live in a time when presidents are called morons (a term applied to George W. Bush, Barack Obama, and Donald Trump) and much worse. But politics has been a rough game for a long time; our earliest presidents were attacked as "pusillanimous," "dastardly," and "contemptible."

The prototypical insult is speech or action that expresses contempt or derision. It can be a gesture: the middle finger or the cuckold sign (formed by extending the index and little fingers).

It can be a drawing, such as Garry Trudeau's depictions of Bill Clinton as a waffle and George W. Bush as an asterisk under an empty cowboy hat. It can be a single phrase or even just a word (usually a noun such as *buffoon, fascist, dotard,* or *cretin*). It can be an assertion (such as Salmon P. Chase's observation that "Grant is a man of vile habits, and of no ideas"), a harsh description (Joseph P. Kennedy's characterization of Franklin Roosevelt as a "crippled son-of-a-bitch"), or something more oblique (Lyndon Johnson's observation that Gerald Ford "played too much football with his helmet off").

First, however, I include some comments about how insults—political insults specifically—work as a genre of verbal behavior.

Disrespect Is in the Eye of the Beholder

An insult is different from a criticism. You might be critical of a public figure—of anyone really—without insulting that person. When Tennessee senator Bob Corker said, "The president has not yet been able to demonstrate the stability, nor some of the competence that he needs to demonstrate in order to be successful," he was critiquing Donald Trump, not insulting him. Trump may have been offended by Corker's remarks, but being offended is different from being insulted. The intention to disrespect or demean is key to insulting someone.

Of course, intentions are often in the eye of the beholder, so the distinction between being insulted and feeling insulted tends to get blurry and to blur the distinction between critique and insult. But not always; a few months later, when Corker referred to the White House as an "adult day-care center," the intention to insult was clear.

Setting, tone, and harshness of language often separate an insult from a criticism or disagreement. A political adversary may dispute a claim in any number of ways, but the person who shouts "You lie!" in the middle of a speech is delivering an insult. That's what South Carolina representative Joe Wilson did when Barack Obama was giving his 2009 State of the Union Address. Wilson's breach of decorum—in effect calling the president a liar—was condemned by members of both parties, and he apologized for his "lack of civility." Wilson was denouncing the president by interrupting with a public condemnation. Not every rebuke or condemnation counts as an insult, but Wilson's shouting, interrupting, and disrespectful language made the comment an insult, not simply an expression of disagreement. The vehemence and tone of Wilson's "You lie!" established an intent and turned the rebuke into an insult.

Intent also allows neutral terms to be perceived as insults, especially when there is an audience prepared to take them that way. We see this with the repositioning of words such as *liberal*, *feminist*, *evangelical*, and *corporate* as terms of abuse. This is the case also with so-called racial and ethnic dog whistles, coded characterizations that play to prejudices. When former senator Bob Kerrey referred to candidate "Barack Hussein Obama" and said that he liked the fact that "his father was a Muslim and that his paternal grandmother is a Muslim," he was ostensibly making a neutral or even positive observation. But in the context of rumors that Obama was a secret Muslim planning to bring jihad to the United States, the comment was a dog whistle. Kerrey later wrote to Obama, explaining, "I answered a question about your qualifications to be president in a way that has been interpreted as a backhanded insult of you."

Sometimes just a well-placed adverb can be enough to craft an insult. You may recall the exchange between Senators Hillary Clinton and Barack Obama at a 2008 New Hampshire debate. When the moderator asked Clinton why people found Obama more likable, she responded with a joke. "Well, that hurts my feelings," she said. "He's very likable. I agree with that. I don't think I'm that bad." Candidate Obama interjected, "You're likable enough, Hillary." The word "enough," coupled with Obama's deadpan delivery, turned the comment into a jibe.

Even a simple party label can be turned around. In the 1960 presidential election, after Richard Nixon had called John F. Kennedy an "economic ignoramus" and a "Pied Piper," Kennedy quipped, "I just confine myself to calling him a Republican, but he says that is getting low."

Intent can also turn an apparent insult into something less. Nixon once described Dwight Eisenhower as "more complex and devious than most people realized." He said he meant it as a compliment. And Douglas MacArthur referred to Harry Truman as a "little bastard." In context, though, MacArthur's comment was part insult and part compliment: "You know, he is a man of raw courage and guts—the little bastard honestly believes he is a patriot."

A Slap in the Face or a Knife in the Back

Insults are often calculated to mock, shame, and anger a target, but also to create a memorable impression for an audience. Attention to parallelism, imagery, rhythm, and sound can make an audience chuckle and the person insulted squirm; examples are "a cheese-paring of a man," "a chameleon on plaid," "a blighted burr," "wish-washy, namby-pamby," and "a flip-flopper."

As public language, political insults create or reinforce negative perceptions (or misperceptions), such as when John Quincy Adams was called a "pimp" or Franklin Roosevelt "a Communist." Since insults seek to harm, shame, and provoke without evoking sympathy, excessively harsh insults can be seen as unfair, such as calling someone a traitor, invoking a comparison to Hitler, or referring to someone as "dyslexic to the point of near-illiteracy," as Christopher Hitchens once described George W. Bush.

Insults may also serve as a means of establishing social or rhetorical dominance, as in the case of flyting, battle rap, or middle school wordplay. The person making an insult challenges the self-worth of the target and symbolically asserts the right to judge. And sometimes insults serve a therapeutic function, expressing anger or frustration and letting another person know just how you feel at a particular moment. When Senator Bob Dole called George H. W. Bush a "fucking Nazi" after being excluded from a 1980 debate, his angry comment combined an insult—the characterizing of his fellow war veteran as a Nazi—with an expression of rage—the adjective *fucking*.

Part of the context of an insult is the way in which it is delivered. Insults can be made in person, for example on a debate stage. But more often political insults occur as public statements in the media, at rallies, or at conventions. They may be intended as a slap in the face, such as when Thomas Paine wrote an open letter to President George Washington calling him "treacherous" and much more. Insults may be intended to whip up the crowd, such as Donald Trump's reference to "Crooked Hillary" at rallies during the 2016 campaign. Some insults are intended as zingers: laugh lines not intended to be taken seriously but designed to be repeated by the media, for example, Patrick Buchanan's 1992 comment that "Bill Clinton's foreign policy experience is pretty much confined to having had breakfast once at the International House of Pancakes." Some insults require a trip to the dictionary. When Teddy Roosevelt called Woodrow Wilson "a Byzantine logothete," journalists had to look up the word to find out that the logothetes of Byzantium were auditors of accounts—literally, accountants.

While many insults appear in speeches, editorials, endorsements, and campaign literature, still others may be public-private communications: quiet, cutting remarks to a confidant intended to make their way into the history books. A few insults are private remarks inadvertently made public, as was the case with Thomas Jefferson's 1795 letter to his friend Philip Mazzei in which he spoke poorly of Washington and Adams. Mazzei shared the letter with others, and it ended up in newspapers, much to Jefferson's embarrassment.

Recurring Themes

The method of conveying presidential insults has changed over the centuries, from using party-funded newspapers to partisan cable news and radio, from private letters to emails, from pamphlets and tavern talk to posts and tweets. Through it all, presidential insults show recurring themes, including too little intellect or too much, inconsistency or obstinacy, worthlessness, weakness, dishonesty, personality flaws, sexual impropriety, and appearance. The semantic categories called out in insults suggest what is hurtful culturally, and insults reveal society's changing prejudices and enduring ones as well. How we insult presidents tells us about the presidents, but it also tells us about the American nation's anxieties and aspirations.

From the characterizations of John Adams as "hermaphroditic" and Martin Van Buren as "womanish" to George H. W. Bush as a "wimp" and Barack Obama as "a pussy," homophobic insults about gender seem to be pervasive. Race and origin are recurring themes. References to lying and hypocrisy are common, sometimes citing character flaws and sometimes political expediency. We find fakes, fakers, and fakirs; the Janus-faced; confidence men; phonies; pettifoggers; mountebanks; charlatans; quacks; and chameleons.

Along with being called liars, presidents have been characterized as weak-willed nonentities. There have been cyphers, tools, dupes, errand boys, frontmen, stooges, and a marionette show's worth of puppets. One was called "a human smudge." Another was referred to as "a flubdub with a streak of the second-rate and the common in him," and still another as "a triumph of lowest-common-denominator politics." Many presidents have been called traitors to their principles and some have been called traitors to their country as well. There have been bullies and clowns, despots, demagogues, and usurpers, radicals and racists, drunkards and cowards. The animal world too is a rich source of characterizations, with a veritable menagerie of hyenas, fat old bulls and stalled oxes, sad jellyfish and angleworms, crows, curs, lapdogs, reptiles, gorillas, baboons, and monkeys. Such uncomplimentary animal metaphors dehumanize presidents while simultaneously caricaturing them.

Linguistic Types and Rhetorical Functions

Insults come in a range of linguistic types and rhetorical functions. Some involve just a word, such as National Security Adviser Brent Scowcroft's characterization of Richard Nixon as a "shit." The lone expletive does all the work.

Often, however, an insult is intensified by modifiers. It can be a matter of simple repetition, as in publisher William Loeb's characterization of candidate Eugene McCarthy as "a skunk's skunk's skunk." However, intensification is most often implemented with descriptive adjectives before the noun. Calling someone a "dictator" or a "tyrant" can be taken as an insult, but referring to a "lawless dictator" or a "besotted tyrant" makes the intention more specific and has more impact. The more adjectives, it seems, the more intensification: Republican Barry Goldwater referred to Richard Nixon as a "two-fisted, four-square liar." To simply call Nixon a liar would be one thing, but the "two-fisted" and "four-square" provide a verbal (and arithmetical) intensification. Harry Truman called Nixon a liar too, but he shifted the characterization to the adjective position, calling Nixon "a no good lying bastard," packing three separate insults into just a few words.

Multiple adjectives can be used to reinforce an impression, piling on related negatives, such as the description of Benjamin Harrison as "a cold-blooded, narrow-minded, prejudiced, obstinate, timid old psalm-singing Indianapolis politician." At other times, the adjectives go every which way, creating a verbal flurry, such as when candidate Bill Clinton was dubbed "a draft-dodging, pro-gay greenhorn, married to a radical feminist."

Such complex phrasings allow insults to be linked together, casting a wide net. Generalities may be tied to specifics, facts to interpretation: calling George H. W. Bush "a Pekingese curled around the ankles of China's tyrants" links his previous ambassadorship and internationalism (specifics) with the image of an approval-seeking pet (a general, dismissive characterization). The naming of the species Pekingese provides additional reinforcement and a touch of snark. Parallelism too can play a role in intensification: Hunter S. Thompson's reference to Richard Nixon as "a swine of a man and a jabbering dupe of a president" differentiates the person ("a swine") and the job performance ("a dupe"). Thompson is able to double up the invective and double down on the insult.

Insults are often intensified using comparisons. Whig congressman Davy Crockett ("the King of the Wild Frontier") called Martin Van Buren "secret, sly, selfish, cold, calculating, distrustful, [and] treacherous," but he finished off that particular insult with the comparison that Van Buren was "as different from Jackson as dung from diamonds."

Comparisons draw on linguistic frames, such as "X is no more than a _____," "X has no more backbone [brains, etc.] than a _____," "X is worse than _____," and "If X was a _____, he would be _____." Framing can be implied as well and can allow a speaker to deliver an insult as a mini-story; Lyndon Johnson's speechwriter, Harry McPherson, described John F. Kennedy as "the enviably attractive nephew who sings an Irish ballad for the company, and then winsomely disappears before the table-clearing and dishwashing begin." The story lets the listener enjoy a moment of discovery when the insult becomes apparent.

Comparisons need not be that complex; they may simply invoke a known reference point, such as Ronald Reagan being called "Herbert Hoover with a smile." Such minimally framed comparisons again allow listeners to infer the insults and unravel the puzzle.

Double meaning and irony have roles as well. Lincoln was called a "presidential pigmy," which had a different impact than the same characterization of diminutive James Madison. Dwight Eisenhower referred to John F. Kennedy as the "young genius," suggesting that perhaps he was not the latter. Serendipity and rhyme are factors: the J of Johnson allowed both Lyndon and Andrew to become "Judas Johnson." We find the evocative Martin Van Ruin, Fainting Frank Pierce, Dishonest Abe Lincoln, Useless Grant, Rutherfraud Hayes, Tricky Dick Nixon, and Slick Willy Clinton. Other insulting names are less memorable: General Mum, Grandfather's Hat, President Caligula.

Freshness is helpful as well. An insult can be memorable when a vivid metaphor or image is created, such as when Herbert Hoover was called a "spineless cactus." The phrase is a semi-oxymoron, invoking both feckless prickliness and the ineptness of a cactus without needles. Theodore Roosevelt relied on parallelism of meaning when he referred to Benjamin Harrison as "the little gray man in the White House." The white of White House provides a contrast that makes poor, gray Harrison seem even dingier. Insults can be mean-spirited, crude, and simple, but in many cases they exhibit the characteristics of poetry: freshness, metaphor, rhyme, and imagery. And like poetry, insults can be a joy to observe and to create, a form of crafted wordplay evoking emotion, appreciation, and insight.

Our Freedom to Insult

It is a common, and very human, response to be stung by insults. Yet presidents and politicians recognize that being insulted is part of their profession. Almost all presidents brood in private about the insults aimed at them. George Washington complained about press "outrages on common decency." Richard Nixon kept an enemies list. Grover Cleveland responded to one satirical article with the comment: "I don't think that there ever was a time when newspaper lying was so general and so mean as at present."

All presidents may share Cleveland's view, but many bear insults gracefully and stoically, and a few even respond with wit and humor. John Tyler reacted to the Whig Manifesto kicking him out of that party with a note to its author, a novelist, telling him that he should stick to writing "romances." Gerald Ford tried to co-opt *Saturday Night Live* by allowing his press secretary to host the show and even had himself taped saying the opening catchphrase, "Live from New York . . . It's *Saturday Night*."

Some presidents can't resist returning insults with invective of their own. When a friendly Southern crowd shouted that Andrew Johnson's critics should be hanged, he responded, "Why not hang them?" Johnson's comments were entered as evidence in his impeachment trial.

Not all presidents suggest the gallows, but many strike back verbally: Henry Adams was called a "little emasculated mass of inanities," Westbrook Pegler was a "rat" and a "guttersnipe," and Joseph Alsop was "the lowest form of animal life on the planet." Some presidents have even responded to insults with legal action. Teddy Roosevelt had William Randolph Hearst's to Joseph Pulitzer's *New York World* prosecuted for libel. Roosevelt lost. More than a century earlier, critics of John Adams were jailed under the short-lived Alien and Sedition Acts, and Thomas Jefferson's allies indicted the publisher of the New York *Wasp* for libel. Today, Donald Trump characterizes reporting he does not like as "fake news" and has called the mainstream press "enemies of the people."

Part of the genius of American democracy—both in our legal system and in our politics—is that citizens can openly insult the president. We enjoy protections of freedom of speech and freedom of the press that other nations do not, and our freedoms allow us to direct invective at the president with legal impunity.

Our Changing Language

Insults tell us about our presidents. They tell us about our values and our history. And they tell us about our language. While the semantic categories of presidential invective are more stable than not, vocabulary evolves, and terms of abuse come and go. New to the twentieth century were *moron*, *jerk*, *asshole*, and *flip-flopper*. Mostly gone were *apostate*, *mountebank*, *flathead*, *doughface*, *dotard*, and *hermaphrodite*. Some insults, such as *puzzlewit*, seem to have never caught on. Others, such as *gink*, quickly came and went; Warren Harding called Herbert Hoover "the smartest gink I know," using a slang term that could, according to the *Oxford English Dictionary* (*OED*), simply mean a fellow but might also refer to someone who is "unworldly or socially inept."

And then there are terms that seem quaint today but were more pointed in their time. On learning that Andrew Jackson hoped that the "old lying scamp" John Quincy Adams would be paralyzed by a stroke, I was puzzled. "Scamp," to me, had the nuance of an unruly neighbor kid. But in Jackson's time, I learned, a scamp was "a good-for-nothing, worthless person, a ne'er-do-well, 'waster.'" Jackson did not see Adams as a modern-day imp, but as a scoundrel.

Words such as *scamp*, together with the iconography of the American Revolution and our reverence for the founders and other historical figures, may mislead us. To many, today's political climate appears to be uniquely toxic and hate-filled, and we may idealize the past as a more genteel and civil era of classical rhetoric and high-minded debate. Such an idealization would be a grave error, as we will presently see. Personal insults and political invective go back a long way.

What Is an Insult?

Insults are symbolic expressions—remarks or actions—that treat someone with scornful abuse or contempt.

Insults occur in a wide range of linguistic and extralinguistic types, from single words to narratives and from artful to crude.

Insults are ad hominem attacks, different from mere criticism in that they are directed at someone's character, intelligence, or person.

The language of an insult does not need to be inherently abusive. Its message relies on context, tone, and audience.

Insults occur in a wide range of contexts, from direct personal insults to public attacks to private comments.

"Old Muttonhead"

TWO

Founders, 1788–1824

John Trumbull's painting *Declaration of Independence* depicts the presentation of the declaration to the Second Continental Congress. The date was June 28, 1776; the place, the Pennsylvania State House. The thirteen colonies had been at war with the British since the battles of Lexington and Concord in April of the previous year.

In Trumbull's painting, Thomas Jefferson is placing the first draft before John Hancock, president of the Congress. Together with Jefferson are the other drafters: John Adams, Roger Sherman, Robert Livingston, and Benjamin Franklin. Less than a week later, on July 4, 1776, the Declaration of Independence was adopted.

The painting is one of four by Trumbull hanging in the Capitol rotunda in Washington, D.C. Two others depict decisive events of the War of Independence: the surrender of General Burgoyne in 1777 and the surrender of Lord Cornwallis in 1781. The fourth is Trumbull's portrait *General George Washington Resigning His Commission*. Washington stands before the president of the Congress, Thomas Mifflin, and hands him a letter of resignation as commander in chief of the Continental Army in December 1783.

Declaration of Independence, by John Trumbull (1818)

Future presidents Thomas Jefferson, James Madison, and James Monroe are among the onlookers.

Declaration of Independence and *Washington Resigning His Commission* are part of the iconography of the War of Independence. In each, documents are exchanged in the presence of serious witnesses. Even the surrenders of Burgoyne and Cornwallis are civil affairs, depicting American leaders treating their opponents as gentlemen.

Looking at these paintings, you might expect that our young nation's political landscape was orderly and civilized, much different from the present era of scorched-earth politics. But in actuality, such civility never existed. Once the new nation was established, divisions arose, and politics became personal and mean. Even George Washington, almost universally popular, was not immune.

Old Muttonhead (George Washington, 1789–1797)

After resigning his military commission, Washington presided over the Constitutional Convention in 1787. With the unanimous support of the electoral college, he was elected president of the new United States in 1788 and re-elected in 1792, with John Adams as his vice president both times. Adams, however, had a so-so opinion of the president, and, in a letter to Benjamin Rush in 1807, stated that Washington "could not write a sentence without misspelling some word."

"could not write a sentence without misspelling some word"

During his presidency, Washington found himself the target of Thomas Paine, whose 1776 pamphlet *Common Sense* had been one of the essential documents of independence. Paine had since moved to France and became a political enemy of Maximilien Robespierre, who had him imprisoned in 1793 as a citizen of Britain, then at war with France.

The US minister to France, Gouverneur Morris, declined to assert Paine's US citizenship, and Paine remained in prison for nearly a year. Paine blamed Morris and Washington for his imprisonment, and after his release he wrote an eight-thousand-word letter to Washington on February 22, 1795—Washington's birthday. Paine's letter began politely, explaining, "The dangers to which I have been exposed cannot have been unknown to you, and the guarded silence you have observed upon that circumstance is what I ought not to have expected from you, either as a friend or as President of the United States."

Paine received no reply; a year later, he gave up the pretense of civility. He published an even longer document, a pamphlet titled *Letter to George Washington, president of the United States of America: On affairs public and private.* It included the earlier letter and much more, including this critique of Washington's leadership: "No wonder we see so much pusillanimity in the President, when we see so little enterprise in the General!" Discussing relations with France, Paine wrote that the "ingratitude" and "pusillanimity of Mr. Washington, and the Washington faction, . . . has brought upon America the loss of character she now suffers in the world." As for Washington personally, Paine remarked: "And as to you, Sir, treacherous in private friendship (for so you have been to me, and that in the day of danger) and a hypocrite in public life, the world will be puzzled to decide whether you are an apostate or an impostor; whether you have abandoned good principles, or whether you ever had any."

Paine vented his frustration in terms that went directly to Washington's image as a careful, honest leader. Earlier in his letter, Paine was no kinder, referring to Washington's "pretensions," to the "fraudulent light" of his character, and to his "nondescribable, chameleon-colored . . . prudence [which is], in many cases, a substitute for principle." Washington dismissed Paine's pamphlet and similar criticism as pro-French propaganda, and he never responded directly to Paine. But he was no doubt insulted.

Paine was not the only American revolutionary sympathetic to the French Revolution and worried about Federalism tilting toward a British-style monarchy. Thomas Jefferson and James Monroe, both former ministers to France, along with James Madison, were anti-Federalist leaders from Virginia, and their private correspondence was sometimes critical of Washington, Hamilton, and Adams and what they saw as an abandonment of the agrarian tradition.

In 1793, Jefferson resigned from Washington's cabinet to lead the Democratic-Republican Party. A bit later, in 1796, Jefferson happened to write a long letter to Philip Mazzei, a former Virginia neighbor living in Italy. After dispensing with some business, Jefferson answered Mazzei's query about politics, writing that "an Anglican, monarchical and aristocratical party has sprung up" and adding: "It would give you a fever were I to name to you the apostates who have gone over to these heresies, men who were Samsons in the field and Solomons in the council, but who have had their heads shorn by the harlot England." Mazzei shared copies of that paragraph on politics with others, and it appeared in 1797 in the Paris *Gazette Nationale ou Le Moniteur Universel* and later in American newspapers.

Jefferson was usually careful not to criticize Washington directly or publicly. Instead he relied on surrogate polemicists such as Philip Freneau. Freneau ran the short-lived *National Gazette*, which he edited while employed by Jefferson's State Department. The paper was intended as a counterbalance to the Federalist *Gazette of the United States*, which supported Hamilton. In addition to criticizing Hamilton's policies, the *National Gazette* described Washington's sixty-first birthday celebration as "a forerunner of other monarchical vices."

Freneau's newspaper ceased publication soon after Jefferson resigned from the State Department, and the chief Republican paper became the Philadelphia *Aurora*, published by Benjamin Franklin Bache, the grandson of the kite-flier. After Washington's farewell address, which warned against political parties, a pseudonymous letter penned by *Aurora* staffer William Duane called it the "loathings of a sick mind."

Sensitive to criticism, in a July 21, 1793, letter to Henry Lee, Washington wrote that he viewed Bache's publications as "arrows of malevolence" and as "outrages on common decency." Washington was insulted.

SAID OF

Washington

"l'assassin"—A surrender document signed by Washington during a battle of the French and Indian War (1754–1763) referred to Washington as "l'assassin" of Joseph Coulon de Villiers de Jumonville in an ambush in 1754. The assassin charges were recycled later in Washington's career.

"a weak general"—Thomas Conway, in 1777, angling to have Washington replaced.

"old muttonhead"—John Adams. Adams added that Washington had "not been found out only because he kept his mouth shut," implying that Washington hid his lack of knowledge behind a façade of reserve.

"Washington has the ostentation of an eastern bashaw"—Benjamin Franklin Bache, using a rare spelling of "pasha."

"He thinks hard of all, is despotic in every respect, he mistrusts every man, thinks every man a rogue"—Jefferson in 1799, as reported by Joshua Brookes.

"a most miserable politician"—from "The Political Creed of 1795" in Bache's *Aurora*.

"The American nation has been debauched by WASHINGTON"—from a 1796 letter printed in *Aurora*.

"the mask of hypocrisy has been alike worn by a CAESAR, a CROMWELL, and a WASHINGTON"—the pseudonymous Scipio, in *Aurora*.

"His mind was great and powerful, without being of the very first order; . . . It was slow in operation, being little aided by invention or imagination, but sure in conclusion"—a backhanded compliment by Jefferson in an appreciation of Washington written in 1814.

His Rotundity (John Adams, 1797–1801)

John Adams and Thomas Jefferson contested the 1796 presidential election, along with Thomas Pinckney and Aaron Burr. As the election unfolded, the partisan press—the new media of its time—was in full swing, with newspapers referring to Adams as a monarchist and Jefferson as a radical. Writers character-

> "one of the most egregious fools on the continent"

ized Adams's "sesquipedality of belly" (alluding to the character Dr. Slop in Laurence Sterne's *Tristram Shandy*) and shared reports that a Southern senator had called the vice president "His Rotundity." Adams won the election narrowly. Until 1808, the vice president was the candidate with the second most electoral votes, so Jefferson was elected to that role.

Foreign policy dominated Adams's administration and led to the Alien and Sedition Acts of 1798, which restricted immigration and made it a crime to publish statements critical of the government. France and England had been at war since 1793, and the 1795 Jay Treaty of Amity between England and the United States infuriated the French. Franco-American hostilities escalated to an undeclared naval war. After rumors of a French conspiracy to attack Philadelphia, Adams won passage of the Alien and Sedition Acts, under which the government prosecuted twenty-six individuals, mostly editors of newspapers critical of the Adams administration.

The first prosecution was of Vermont congressman Matthew Lyon, who accused Adams of having "an unbounded thirst for ridiculous pomp." Also jailed were Benny Bache and James Callendar. Bache's paper had referred to Adams as "old, querulous, bald, blind, crippled [and] toothless." Callendar was the scandalmonger who in 1797 had published the story of Alexander Hamilton's affair with Maria Reynolds and had also accused Hamilton of using Treasury Department funds to cover it up. Jefferson hired him to attack Adams in the 1796 election.

In his booklet *The Prospect before Us,* Callender collected a series of essays in which he wrote that Adams was a "repulsive pedant" and more. He rounded it all out with a reference to Adams's "hideous hermaphroditical character, which has neither the force and firmness of a man, nor the gentleness and sensibility of a woman." He was referring here to Adams's character, not his gender identity, but even in 1800, political insults were sexualized.

Republican journalists such as Bache and Callender were not the only ones attacking Adams. Adams continued to be condemned as a monarchist and was even accused of trying to marry off one of his daughters to a son of King George III so that he could establish a royal dynasty. In the fall of 1800, Alexander Hamilton wrote a fourteen-thousand-word pamphlet attacking Adams, stating, among other things, that "there are great and intrinsic defects in his character, which unfit him for the office of Chief Magistrate." He called Adams "an ordinary man [who] dreams himself to be a Frederick [the Great]" and whose "vanity" leads him to "fall into the hands of miserable intriguers, with whom his self-love is more at ease."

John Adams despised his fellow Federalist, referring to Hamilton as "devoid of every moral principle—a bastard and as much a foreigner as [Albert] Gallatin," the Swiss-born congressman. And in an 1806 letter to Benjamin Rush, Adams called Hamilton "a bastard brat of a Scotch pedlar!" Many years later, after Hamilton's death, Adams published a line-by-line response to the latter's pamphlet.

Bad Ware (Thomas Jefferson, 1801–1809)

Adams was ambivalent about Jefferson, recognizing him as talented but ambitious. In a 1793 letter to his wife, Abigail, Adams wrote that "instead of being the ardent pursuer of science that some think him, I know he is indolent, and his soul

"a dastardly poltroon"

is poisoned with Ambition." In a January 1794 letter, Adams recounted that "Jefferson went off Yesterday, and a good riddance of bad ware. I hope his Temper will be more cool and his Principles more reasonable in Retirement than they have been in office. I am almost tempted to wish he may be chosen Vice President at the next Election for there if he could do no good, he could do no harm."

In the election of 1800, Jefferson was portrayed as a radical who would bring the violence of the French Revolution to the United States. Jefferson's enthusiasm for the French Jacobins prompted the *Connecticut Courant* to worry that if he were elected, "Murder, robbery, rape, adultery, and incest will be openly taught and practiced, the air will be rent with the cries of the distressed, the soil will be soaked with blood, and the nation black with crimes." John Mason's *The Voice of Warning to Christians on the Ensuing Election* attacked Jefferson as an atheist who "writes against the truths of God's words; who makes not even a profession of Christianity; who is without Sabbaths; without the sanctuary, and without so much as a decent external respect for the faith and worship of Christians." Supporters of Adams also spread the rumor that Jefferson was dead.

The Federalists were in disarray, however, and Adams and Charles Pinckney lost the 1800 election. Yet Jefferson's victory was anything but simple. The Democratic-Republican candidates Jefferson and Burr tied in electoral votes, and the House of Representatives only awarded Jefferson the election on the thirty-sixth ballot.

Perhaps the contested election was a sign of troubles to come. Jefferson's hatchet man Callendar soon turned on him. Callendar had been jailed during the Adams administration, and upon his release he expected a government post. When Jefferson ignored him, Callendar publicized Jefferson's relationship with Sally Hemings. In the September 1, 1802, issue of the *Richmond Recorder*, Callendar wrote: "It is well known that the man, whom it delighteth the people to honor, keeps, and for many years past has kept, as his concubine, one of his own slaves. Her name is SALLY. The name of her eldest son is TOM. His features are said to bear a striking resemblance to the President himself." A spate of racist commentary came from the Federalist newspapers and others, including mocking poems and cartoons. Jefferson managed to ignore the revelations, as did historians until the late twentieth century. And while Jefferson was publicly supportive of the free press, he quietly supported state prosecutions of a few newspapers to set an example. In 1803, when Harry Croswell, the editor of the *Wasp*, referred to Jefferson as "a dissembling patriot" and a "pretended 'man of the people,'" he was convicted by a New York court of seditious libel.

Jefferson's administration was also marked by controversy over federal power. When the treaty approving the Louisiana Purchase was debated, Congressman Manasseh Cutler called Jefferson "as despotic as the Grand Turk."

Nor was any love lost between Jefferson and his first vice president, Aaron Burr. Jefferson blocked Burr's renomination in 1804, after which Burr alluded to Jefferson as a demagogue in his farewell speech to the Senate: "It is here in this exalted refuge—here, if anywhere, will be resistance made to the storms of political frenzy and the silent arts of corruption. And if the Constitution be destined ever to perish by the sacrilegious hands of the demagogue or the usurper, which God avert, its expiring agonies will be witnessed on this floor."

Burr later become involved in a plot to establish an independent republic in the Southwest and was accused of plotting to assassinate Jefferson. Jefferson declared Burr a traitor in a January 1806 message to Congress, nearly a month before the latter's arrest and indictment, but despite Jefferson's pressure, Burr was acquitted.

SAID OF

Jefferson

"a dastardly poltroon"—John Adams, using an old word for *coward*.

"would make our wives and daughters the victims of legalized prostitution"—Yale president Timothy Dwight, in 1804.

"one of the most detestable of mankind"—Martha Washington.

"a slur upon the moral government of the world"—John Quincy Adams.

a *"contemptible hypocrite"*—Hamilton.

"a confirmed infidel"—Reverend John Mason, a New England preacher.

a *"brandy-soaked defamer of churches"*—attributed to Jefferson's Federalist opponents, who attacked his supposed hostility to Christianity. Connecticut preacher Thomas Robins called Jefferson a "howling atheist."

"disgraces not only the place he fills but produces immorality by his pernicious example"—General Phillip Schuyler, Hamilton's father-in-law, commenting on the 1803 *Croswell* libel case, which Alexander Hamilton argued before the New York Supreme Court. The conviction stood, on a tie vote, but Croswell was never sentenced, and the New York libel laws were changed in 1805.

possessed of *"a weak, wavering, indecisive character,"* fit perhaps *"to be a professor in a College, President of a Philosophical Society, or even Secretary of State; but certainly not the first magistrate of a great nation"*—South Carolina Federalist Robert Goodloe Harper.

the "coward of Carter's Mountain"—the *New York Evening Post*, referring to Jefferson's flight from Monticello in 1781.

Fake News?

Presidents and their supporters have sometimes used libel laws as a tool. The Sedition Act of 1798 provided fines and jail penalties for anyone who "shall write, print, utter or publish . . . false, scandalous and malicious" comments about "the government or the President." As previously mentioned, the administration of John Adams went on to prosecute twenty-six individuals, mostly editors of newspapers critical of the Adams administration.

Thomas Jefferson opposed the Alien and Sedition Acts as federal overreach and was happy to see the Sedition Act expire in 1800. In 1806, two years after the *Croswell* case was decided in the Supreme Court, a federal grand jury in Connecticut returned charges against writers and publishers associated with the *Litchfield Monitor* and the *Connecticut Courant*. The charges arising from the *Courant's* 1806 story accusing Jefferson of secretly bribing Napoleon with sixty tons of silver—about $2 million at the time—resulted in an indictment. The *Connecticut Courant* case, *United States v. Hudson and Goodwin*, went to the US Supreme Court, which decided in 1812 that federal courts did not have jurisdiction over common law offenses such as libel unless Congress specifically passed a law criminalizing them.

A century later, in 1908, Joseph Pulitzer's *New York World* and Indianapolis *News* reported on alleged corruption in the payment of $40 million by the US government to purchase a French company's holdings in Colombia for the Panama Canal. Roosevelt was incensed, and in a special message to Congress, he called the charges "a libel against the United States government" and said of Pulitzer that it was "a high national duty to bring to justice this vilifier of the American people."

Pulitzer's company was indicted on convoluted charges involving national defense. Prosecutors argued that the publications violated an old federal law prohibiting malicious injury to harbor defenses, since the newspaper had been circulated at West Point, federal property. In *United States v. Press Publishing Co.*, the Supreme Court rejected the indictment, noting that "the offense, if any, was committed wholly within the jurisdiction of the State of New York." Pulitzer claimed victory.

During the New Deal era in the 1930s, libel re-emerged as a way of threatening the press. Senator Sherman Minton, whose Senate Special Committee to Investigate Lobbying Activities was investigating the opposition press, proposed a federal libel bill imposing a prison sentence of up to two years for publishing news "known to be false." The bill evoked bipartisan outrage and was soon withdrawn.

In 1964, the Supreme Court finally weighed in definitively on whether public figures could seek damages for libel over errors in reporting. The Montgomery, Alabama, commissioner of public safety sued the *New York Times* and civil rights activists over a full-page advertisement criticizing the actions of police. The Court took the opportunity to establish the standard that in the case of public figures seeking damages for libel, "actual malice" was required rather than mere error. In *New York Times v. Sullivan*, the Court wrote that "erroneous statement is inevitable in free debate" and that "debate on public issues . . . may well include vehement, caustic, and sometimes unpleasantly sharp attacks on government and public officials."

The decision was unanimous.

Little Jemmy (James Madison, 1809–1817)

In 1809, Jefferson was succeeded by Secretary of State James Madison, who would preside over the new nation's first declared war. Britain and France had gone to war in 1803 over control of the Atlantic Ocean. Tensions mounted with

"he is but a withered apple John"

British economic sanctions and as the British pressed American seamen into service on their ships. By April 1812, Congress voted for a British embargo of its own and in June voted for war. The vote in the Senate was divided regionally, with Southern War Hawks eyeing Canada and west Florida and aiming to suppress Indian resistance in the West. New England preferred peace and trade.

The war did not go as hoped, and American forces were defeated in Detroit and near Niagara Falls. Under the leadership of Oliver Perry, William Henry Harrison, and Andrew Jackson, Americans won victories in Canada and the Mississippi Territory, including the tragic Battle of Horseshoe Bend (1814). In 1814, the British went on the offensive again, raiding ports, occupying parts of Maine, and even burning the White House.

A peace treaty was signed on Christmas Eve 1814, though word of the treaty did not reach the United States in time to stop the Battle of New Orleans (1815). But soon "Mr. Madison's War," as it was referred to, came to an end.

Madison's reputation went up and down with the war effort, but he faced particular opposition from New England's Federalists, whose Hartford Convention discussed the merits of secession. His most persistent press critic was Alexander Contee Hanson's *Federal Republican*, which referred to Madison as Napoleon's "humble imitator and submissive satellite" and which decried his "cunning and his habitual deceit and hypocrisy" as well as his "usurpations and tyranny." Madison's conduct of the war faced criticism from War Hawks as well, with House Speaker Henry Clay calling him "wholly unfit for the storms of war."

The presidency weighed heavily on Madison. Writer Washington Irving described Dolley Madison and the five-foot-four-inch president this way in an 1811 letter: "Mrs. Madison is a fine, portly, buxom dame—who has a smile & pleasant word for every body. Her sisters, Mrs. Cutts & Mrs. Washington, are like two merry wives of Windsor; but as to Jemmy Madison—ah! poor Jemmy!, he is but a withered apple John." Dolley Madison did not escape unscathed, however. She had acted as Jefferson's social secretary during his administration and was attacked in the partisan press in 1808 with rumors that she had had affairs with Jefferson and others.

Like Jefferson, Madison tried to ignore the press and political criticism, even the calls for secession and impeachment, and after peace was concluded, he was able to see his secretary of war, James Monroe, ascend to the presidency.

 SAID OF

Madison

"a [weak] feeble and pusillanimous spirit"—Virginia congressman John Randolph, leader of the "Old Republicans."

a man of "cool and insidious moderation"—Randolph.

"a gloomy, stiff creature"—Martha Daingerfield Bland, the wife of Colonel Theoderick Bland.

"a plain and rather mean-looking little man, of great simplicity of manners"—Francis James Jackson, the British envoy to Washington from 1809 to 1811, on the eve of the War of 1812.

Jefferson's "political pimp"—the *Federal Republican* in 1812.

"a book politician" who "seems evidently to want manly firmness and energy of character"—Fisher Ames, Federalist congressman from Massachusetts.

"timid and indecisive as a statesman"—Pennsylvania Republican leader John Beckley, in a letter to Monroe.

"a mere puppet or cypher managed by some chiefs of the faction behind the curtain"—Federalist Samuel Taggert.

"Whiffling Jemmy"—Alexander Hanson, editor of the *Federal Republican*.

a "Bonaparte"—Hanson.

A Tool of the French (James Monroe, 1817–1825)

Madison's successor in 1817 was James Monroe, Jefferson's other protégé. Monroe had a long history as a politician and diplomat, and his 1796 recall as minister to France became a cause célèbre for Republicans. When Monroe later

"damned infernal old scoundrel"

wrote a pamphlet defending himself, George Washington scribbled extensive marginalia in a copy of the work, noting at one point that "there is abundant evidence of his being a mere tool in the hands of the French government; cajoled & led away always by unmeaning assuran[ce]s of Friends."

Monroe served as governor of Virginia, and Jefferson later appointed him as minister to France and then England. But Jefferson was disappointed in Monroe's negotiations with the British in 1806, declining to send the Monroe-Pinckney Treaty to the Senate for ratification, and in 1808, the *Alexandria Gazette* characterized Monroe as being "in disgrace with the old man in the mountain."

The friendship between Monroe and Madison also cooled for a time. In 1808 a group of Republicans known as the Tertium Quids had supported Monroe over Madison in the nominating caucus. Yet when Madison fired the ineffectual Robert Smith in 1811, he turned to Monroe as secretary of state. Monroe later also served as Madison's secretary of war during the final crucial months of the War of 1812. Despite some grumblings about still another

Virginian running for president, he was well positioned to win the Republican nomination over Georgia's William Crawford.

Among those unimpressed with Monroe's candidacy was Aaron Burr, who said in a letter to his son-in-law: "The man himself is one of the most improper and incompetent that could have been selected—naturally dull and stupid—extremely illiterate—indecisive to a degree that would be incredible to one who did not know him—pusillanimous and of course hypocritical."

Monroe easily defeated Rufus King in the election of 1816. He launched a national unity tour to win over Federalists, and even the newspapers in Boston were impressed, one proclaiming an "era of Good Feelings." Monroe ran unopposed in 1820 and was re-elected with all but one of the 232 electoral votes. Nevertheless, Monroe faced such challenges as responding to the panic of 1819, when postwar growth stalled, and whether slavery should be permitted in new states added to the Union. The latter issue resulted in the Missouri Compromise of 1820, which linked the entry of slave states and free states.

 SAID OF

Monroe

"a liar"—Hamilton, with whom Monroe nearly fought a duel. Monroe replied that Hamilton was "a scoundrel."

"weak & vain"—Washington, in his marginalia.

a *"disgraced minister, recalled in displeasure for misconduct"*—John Adams in 1797, complaining about Monroe's pamphlet defending his diplomatic work.

"Nature has given him a mind neither rapid nor rich"—William Wirt, in 1803. Wirt later became Monroe's attorney general.

a *"fawning parasite"*—the *Alexandria Gazette.*

a *"damned infernal old scoundrel"*—Treasury Secretary William Crawford in a meeting with Monroe.

"a dull, sleepy, insignificant-looking man"—publisher and author Samuel Griswold Goodrich.

"He hasn't got brains enough to hold his hat on"—overheard by Goodrich at the White House in February 1825.

"There is slowness, want of decision and a spirit of procrastination in the President, which perhaps arises more from his situation than his personal character"—John Quincy Adams, Monroe's secretary of state, offering a backhanded defense of Monroe's style.

The War of 1812 and the Monroe administration ushered in a new generation of political leaders, and a new generation of insults was coming as well.

ETYMOLOGICAL EXPLORATIONS

Pusillanimous pussyfooters

Pusillanimous was one of the favorite insults of Thomas Paine and other early Americans, and it is still used even today to provide a touch of polysyllabic erudition to an insult.

In the 1970s, speechwriter Pat Buchanan put the phrase *pusillanimous pussyfooters* on the lips of Vice President Spiro Agnew to refer to critics of the Nixon administration's war policy. The alliteration might suggest a common etymology, but that is not the case. *Pusillanimous* comes from the Latin word *pusillus* (meaning weak or very small; it is the diminutive of *pullus*, the word for the young of an animal). *Pusillus* combines with *animus*, meaning spirit or mind, to yield a compound meaning weakness of spirit.

Pussyfooting comes from the adjective *pussyfooted*, which was used from the late nineteenth century to refer to someone who proceeded with excessive caution—with cat-like steps. The *pussy* of *pussyfooting* has also been used as a female term of endearment from the sixteenth century, later extended by metonymy to genitals and metaphorically to cat-like or feminized males. Etymologically, *pussy* is cognate with such words as Dutch *poes* and Danish *pus* and may have originated as a calling name to attract a cat.

In 1940, Republican candidate Wendell Willkie made headlines by calling his own advisers "timid pussyfooters," and in the 1960 election, vice presidential candidate Henry Cabot Lodge accused John F. Kennedy of "pussyfooting and dodging" issues.

"The Hero of Many a Well-Fought Bottle"

THREE

The Rise of the Common Man, 1824–1860

In the period from 1824 to 1860, ten presidents struggled with the transformation of a still-new nation and its political system. The means of nominating and electing presidents continued to evolve, as did the political parties. The Federalists gave way to the Whigs (and later the Republicans), and the Democratic Party was launched in the tumultuous election of 1828. With the exception of Andrew Jackson, none of the presidents of this period served more than a single term.

Reform movements brought scrutiny to many aspects of society, most notably in the debate over slavery. At the same time, doctrines of Manifest Destiny drove expansion to the west and brought about a controversial war with Mexico. As new states entered the union while old regional interests held reform at bay, violence arose on the horizon.

The Corrupt Bargainer (John Quincy Adams, 1825–1829)

John Quincy Adams came to prominence in his twenties. He served as an ambassador in three of the first four administrations and as Monroe's

"perverse and mulish"

secretary of state, and he was well positioned for the presidency in 1824. An inveterate diarist, Adams wrote this characterization of himself in 1819: "I am a man of reserved, cold, austere and forbidding manners: my political enemies say, a gloomy misanthropist, and my personal enemies, an unsocial savage."

That election of 1824 was a contentious affair, with three other candidates competing: Treasury Secretary William Crawford, House Speaker Henry Clay, and Andrew Jackson, the popular general who had become a senator the year before. The election broke new ground, too, as most states now chose electors by popular vote rather than leaving the choice up to state legislators.

Adams finished second in the electoral vote and the popular vote, about fifty thousand votes behind Jackson. But no candidate received a majority of electoral votes, so the election was thrown into the House of Representatives. With the eventual support of fourth-place-finisher Clay, Adams was named president. Clay was appointed secretary of state in what was called "the Corrupt Bargain." As for Jackson, he resigned from the Senate and dedicated himself to making Adams a one-term president. One newspaper even printed this death notice for the United States itself: "Expired at Washington, on the ninth of February, of poison administered by the assassin hands of John Quincy Adams, usurper, and Henry Clay, the virtue, liberty and independence of the United States."

Adams put forth an agenda of road and canal building, conservation, and education—including the establishment of a national observatory—but was stymied time and again by opponents in Congress. John Randolph, a leader of the "Old Republicans," accused Adams of being a traitor to Republican principles. In a March 1826 speech, Randolph said, "It is my duty to leave nothing undone that I may lawfully do, to pull down this administration. . . . They who, from indifference, or with their eyes open, persist in hugging the traitor to their bosom, deserve to be insulted."

In the election of 1828, Adams was attacked as an immoral, European-style aristocrat, a monarchist with a foreign-born English wife, an out-of-touch intellectual who spoke Latin, and even as a gambler who purchased a billiards table with public funds. Jackson's supporters referred to Adams as "the pimp of the coalition" and "the panderer of an Autocrat," reviving an old story from the *Hampshire Patriot*, whose editor suggested that, as ambassador to Russia, Adams had sent his children's nanny to entertain Tsar Alexander I.

In the end, Jackson made good on his promise to oust Adams. Nevertheless, Adams was elected to the House of Representatives in 1830, serving until his death in 1848 and earning the nickname "Old Man Eloquent."

 SAID OF

John Quincy Adams

Adams's political enemies referred to him as *"King John II,"* and when he was in the House after serving as president, the *Albany Argus* called him *"the Madman of Massachusetts."*

"an apostate"— New York governor DeWitt Clinton referred to the contest between Jackson and Adams as between the "lion and the unicorn" and wrote that Adams was "in politics an apostate, and in private life, a pedagogue and everything but amiable and honest."

"old lying scamp"—As president and afterward, Andrew Jackson dismissed Adams's diplomatic achievements. Learning of Adams's anger at this,

Jackson commented that he hoped the "old lying scamp" would be "stricken down by a paralytic stroke."

"Squintz"—Stratford Canning, the British minister to Washington in the early 1820s, referred to Adams, who had perennial eye problems, using this word.

"clownish"—William Henry Harrison, then a senator from Ohio, remarked in 1817, "It is said that [Adams] is a disgusting man. Coarse, dirty, and clownish in his address and stiff and abstracted in his opinions which are drawn from books exclusively."

"His disposition is as perverse and mulish as that of his father"—James Buchanan, writing to a friend in 1822 about the possible candidates in the next election.

A Man of Violent Temper (Andrew Jackson, 1829–1837)

Orphaned by the Revolutionary War, Andrew Jackson left a legal career for the military and rose to prominence in the War of 1812, serving later as governor of the Florida Territory. Known for his violent temper, to some Jackson was an advocate of the newly enfranchised common

> "a barbarian who could not write a sentence of grammar"

man, and to others, an ignorant opportunist and would-be dictator. By 1824, he was a senator running for president, and in 1828, he did not intend to be beaten again. Jackson's troops had called him Old Hickory for his toughness, and his local political committees, or Hickory Clubs as they were known, succeeded in creating the popular momentum needed to defeat Adams.

Attacks by Adams's supporters played on Jackson's reputation for violence, labeling him a man of "ungoverned temper, inflexible resolution, [and] vindictive spirit," as the *Daily National Journal* phrased it. He was characterized as "blood thirsty" for having fought several duels, including a famous 1806 confrontation in which he was shot in the chest before killing his opponent. Jackson had also ordered men executed during the War of 1812, and one broadside printed by John Binns showed eighteen coffins of militiamen and noncombatants executed at the Battle of Horseshoe Bend (1814). The term *coffin handbill* entered the political lexicon as an early form of political attack.

The political attacks of 1828 also mentioned Jackson's parentage. The *Cincinnati Gazette* published the claim that "General Jackson's mother was a COMMON PROSTITUTE, brought to this country by the British soldiers! She afterwards married a MULATTO MAN, with whom she had several children, of which number General JACKSON IS ONE!!!"

What angered Jackson the most were the attacks on his wife, Rachel, whom pamphlets called a "bigamist" and an "American Jezebel." The two began living together in 1791 and were married in 1794, after Rachel was divorced from Lewis Robards. She claimed abandonment; Robards charged adultery, and the confused domestic situation came up in the 1828 election. One pamphlet asked: "Ought a convicted adulteress and her paramour husband to be placed in the highest offices of this free and Christian land?" The attacks on the Jacksons failed to sway voters, but Rachel Jackson did not live to see her husband inaugurated. She died in December 1828 at the age of sixty-one.

As president, Jackson was often ill. He presided over a cabinet rife with infighting, frequently centered on the competing ambitions of John C. Calhoun and Martin Van Buren. At one point, Jackson dismissed almost his entire cabinet, ostensibly over the snubbing of Peggy Eaton, the wife of the secretary of war. Jackson expanded the power of the presidency with vetoes, with his resolve during the nullification crisis, and by his refusal to fund the Bank of the United States.

Re-elected in 1832, Jackson was later censured by the US Senate for failing to turn over documents related to the bank decision, the Senate rebuking him for assuming "authority and power not conferred by the Constitution." When Democrats regained the majority in the Senate, they had the censure resolution officially expunged from the *Senate Journal*.

SAID OF

Jackson

"a confidence man with his painted woman"—the *Daily National Journal*.

"the Great Western Bluebeard"—the *Massachusetts Journal*, referring to the villain of the French folktale who murdered his wives. Other newspapers supporting Adams called Jackson "the Tennessee Slanderer," "the man of the Pistol and Dirk," and "the fireside Hyena of character."

a *"monster [who] . . . shoots, stabs, roasts, and eats his fellow man"*—John Taliaferro, member of Congress from Virginia, quoted in a coffin handbill. Taliaferro accused Jackson of eating the corpses of slain Indians.

"an ignorant, weak, superannuated man"—Senator Samuel Bell of New Hampshire in 1831. Bell went on to say Jackson was "scarcely [more] fitted for the office he now holds, than a child of ten years would be."

"a man of violent temper and very moderate talents"—Alexis de Tocqueville, who toured America in 1831 and 1832.

"a greater tyrant than Cromwell, Caesar, or Bonaparte"—Congressman David Crockett, in a speech in 1834.

a *"Bully"*—a chant used by Adams's supporters, called "The ABC of Democracy: The Adulteress, the Bully, and the Cuckold." It went this way:

"Oh Andy! Oh Andy!

How many men have you hanged in your life?
How many weddings make a wife?"

"a barbarian"—John Quincy Adams. When Harvard granted an honorary
doctorate of law to Andrew Jackson in 1833, Adams boycotted the event
and complained to Harvard president Josiah Quincy, his cousin, that
Jackson was "a barbarian who could not write a sentence of grammar."

The Little Magician (Martin Van Buren, 1837–1841)

Jackson's first vice president, John C. Calhoun, resigned in protest in December 1832 to return to the Senate. He had been replaced on the ticket earlier that year by Martin Van Buren. Van Buren had worked his way up in New York politics, serving as a senator and

"struts and swaggers like a crow in the gutter"

as New York's governor for just forty-three days before joining Jackson's cabinet as secretary of state. In 1836, Van Buren was nominated by the newly renamed Democratic Party to succeed Old Hickory.

Van Buren's many enemies called him "the Red Fox of Kinderhook," alluding to his hair, his slyness, and his hometown. He was also known as "The Little Magician," and his skills at political intrigue were evident as he outmaneuvered Calhoun in Jackson's cabinet. He ran out of magic as president, however, failing to respond quickly to the panic of 1837 and supporting policies that angered both Northerners and Southerners. Van Buren lost the election of 1840 to William Henry Harrison but would try again in 1844 (losing the Democratic nomination to James Polk) and yet again in 1848 (on the Free Soil Party ticket).

Though he came from a modest background—his father was a Dutch innkeeper—Van Buren was portrayed as aristocratic and foppish. His Whig nemesis was Congressman Davy Crockett, who published a 209-page biography attacking Van Buren's character and masculinity. Crockett wrote that Van Buren was "laced up in corsets, such as women in a town wear, and, if possible, tighter than the best of them. It would be difficult to say, from his personal appearance, whether he was a man or woman, but for his large red and gray whiskers."

An even more devastating attack came from Pennsylvania congressman Charles Ogle, who gave his "Golden Spoon Oration" in Congress in April 1840. Ogle depicted Van Buren as living in a "Presidential palace . . . perhaps not less conspicuous than the King's house in many of the royal capitals of Europe" with "its gorgeous banqueting halls, its sumptuous drawing rooms, its glittering and dazzling saloons."

 SAID OF

Van Buren

"Van Buren is as opposite to Jackson as dung is to a diamond"– Davy Crockett, 1836.

a *"secret, sly, selfish, cold, calculating, distrustful, treacherous [. . .] little man"*–Crockett.

a *"bold, unscrupulous and vindictive demagogue"*–John C. Calhoun.

"He is not . . . of the race of the lion or of the tiger; he belonged to a lower order—the fox"–Calhoun.

He *"struts and swaggers like a crow in the gutter"*–Crockett.

"He is what the English call a dandy"–Crockett.

"an arch scoundrel," "the prince of villains," and *"a confirmed knave"*—DeWitt Clinton, in letters to a friend.

"a crawling reptile, whose only claim was that he had inveigled the confidence of a credulous, blind, dotard, old man"—William Seward, in the 1836 campaign, referring to Jackson as well.

"Martin Van Ruin"—appellation used by Van Buren's opponents during his presidency.

"Van, Van, he's a used-up man"—Whig slogan in the 1840 election.

A Clodhopper (William Henry Harrison, 1841)

The Whigs passed up Henry Clay in 1840 and nominated a sixty-seven-year-old former general as their standard-bearer. William Henry Harrison ran as the candidate of frontier values, emphasizing his somewhat fictionalized log cabin background. In fact, Harrison was the son of a signer of the Declaration of Independence,

> "a weak, vain old man in the dotage of expiring ambition"

whose large family lived in a plantation-style home in Indiana. When his military career ended, Harrison served as a territorial governor, in the House and Senate, and as the minister to Colombia. He lobbied for the vice presidency in 1832, but John Quincy Adams passed him over, writing that Harrison was "not without talents, but self-sufficient [i.e., self-serving], vain, and indiscreet."

In 1836, Harrison was put forward as a regional Whig candidate for president and did better than expected, so in 1840, the national Whig Party rallied around him to defeat Van Buren. Harrison was the first to actively campaign for the office in person, in part to allay fears that he was too old to serve. That didn't stop the Democrats from attacking both his age and his military service, referring to him as "Granny Harrison" and as a "petticoat general," a term for a coward.

The Whigs portrayed Harrison as man of the people, with a taste for hard cider—a contrast to Van Buren's corsets and finger bowls. Philadelphia distiller Edmund Booz even marketed hard cider in log-cabin-shaped bottles, promoting Harrison and associating the name Booz with liquor. "Tippecanoe and Tyler Too" became Harrison's campaign slogan, invoking the battle Harrison had led against Tecumseh near the Tippecanoe River. Hearing the slogan, a Clay supporter described it as having "rhyme but no reason."

Harrison was believed to have few strong political convictions and said very little, which allowed Democrats to attack him as "General Mum." That flexibility also made him attractive to Whigs such as Clay, by then the Senate leader, and Daniel Webster, who became Harrison's secretary of state. The Whig infighting to influence Harrison had just begun when he died, thirty-one days into his term.

SAID OF

William Henry Harrison

"a clodhopper"—Harrison, referring to himself. He wrote to a friend in 1836: "Some folks are silly enough to have formed a plan to make a president out of this clerk and clodhopper."

a "bavard"—John Quincy Adams, using the French term for chatterbox.

"the greatest egotist that ever wrote the English language"—Isaac Crary, a Democratic congressman from Michigan, in a speech in the House.

"a living mass of ruined matter"—the Democratic press, alluding to Harrison's health and age.

"a political adventurer" with *"a lively and active, but shallow mind."*—John Quincy Adams, who appointed Harrison minister to Colombia.

"a weak, vain old man in the dotage of expiring ambition"—the Washington *Globe*, which also called him "a gossiping old lady . . . who lives on a sinecure clerkship in a city but is pretended to be a FARMER living in a log cabin and drinking hard cider."

"the present imbecile chief"—Jackson, who had fired Harrison as minister to Colombia.

"a superannuated and pitiable dotard"—the *Globe*.

ETYMOLOGICAL EXPLORATIONS

Dotards

When North Korean leader Kim Jong-un referred to Donald Trump as a "dotard," he (or his translators) revived an insult from the nineteenth century that had been applied to Andrew Jackson, William Henry Harrison, and James Buchanan. The *OED* gives the etymology as coming from the verb *dote*, meaning to "be silly, deranged, or out of one's wits," and the suffix *-ard*. The *OED* cites fourteenth-century examples from Chaucer that refer to an "olde dotard" and an "olde dotard shrewe," and it defines the word as "a person whose intellect is impaired by age; a person in his or her dotage or second childhood." The *OED* also notes the obsolete sense of "a person who dotes on something."

Dotard will probably soon be relegated back to the crossword-puzzle pages, since the *-ard* ending calls to mind the offensive term *retard*, and it also suggests insensitivity toward age-related disabilities.

The *Globe* referred to Harrison as "a superannuated and pitiable dotard." The meaning of *superannuated* overlaps with that of *dotard*. The word is borrowed from the Latin past participle *superannatus*, meaning "too old."

In English, the verb *superannuate* meant to retire someone with a pension because of age or infirmity, and that meaning has been extended to the sense of declaring someone or something obsolete.

His Accidency (John Tyler, 1841–1845)

A Virginia senator in 1840, John Tyler was put on the ticket with Harrison to attract Southern voters. When Harrison suddenly died, the situation was unprecedented. Harrison's cabinet was beginning to debate whether Tyler should be considered acting president or actual president

"an imbecile in the Executive Chair"

when Tyler resolved the issue by taking the oath of office. He would be the first of several presidents to be referred to as accidental, and Whig newspapers also called him "The Executive Ass."

Born into the Southern planter aristocracy, Tyler had begun his political career as a Democrat and was at odds with much of the Whig agenda. In what was known as the Whig Manifesto, written by Representative John Pendleton Kennedy, the party expelled him, announcing that it was ending its "unnatural relationship" with Tyler. Tyler responded with a note to Kennedy, who was a novelist, saying he should stick to writing "romances." An impeachment bill was also introduced in Congress, the first against a sitting president. Though it was rejected by the House of Representatives, Tyler became a man without a party, and in 1844 the Whigs nominated Henry Clay, while the Democrats picked James K. Polk of Tennessee.

At Jackson's urging, Tyler threw his support to Polk. Tyler retired to Virginia, re-emerging politically in 1861 at a failed peace conference intended to avert the Civil War and finally as a candidate to the Virginia Secession Conference.

 SAID OF

Tyler

"a poor weeping willow of a creature"—Francis Blair, editor of the Washington *Globe*, worrying that Tyler would defer to Senate leader Henry Clay.

"his Accidency"— Senate leader Clay, among others.

"our Polonius president"—John Pendleton Kennedy, alluding to the character in *Hamlet*.

"an imbecile in the Executive Chair"—ex-president Andrew Jackson.

"a political sectarian of the slave-driving Jeffersonian school"—John Quincy Adams, writing in his journal about Tyler's opposition to Whig proposals.

a *"traitor"* to the *Whigs*—Edward Stanley, a Whig Congressman.

"weak & conceited"—British envoy Lord Ashburton, who was negotiating border issues with Tyler's administration.

"a man destitute of intellect and integrity, whose name is the synonym of nihil"—the *Richmond Enquirer*, perhaps playing on Tyler's name and his many vetoes.

a *"renegade"*—Whig posters announcing the burning in effigy of the "renegade, John Tyler" in St. Louis in 1841.

a *"poor imbecile"*—the Reverend Joshua Leavitt, editor of the antislavery journal the *Emancipator*.

"mad, weak & a traitor"—North Carolina senator Willie P. Mangum, one of the founders of the Whig Party.

"irrational"—Henry Clay, in an 1841 Senate speech, referring to Tyler's veto of the bank bill.

a "poor unfortunate deluded old jackass"—George Templeton Strong, when the fifty-four-year-old Tyler married twenty-one-year-old Julia Gardiner. The couple would go on to have seven children, bringing the total of Tyler's offspring to fifteen.

The Dark Horse (James K. Polk, 1845–1849)

James K. Polk was the first dark-horse candidate. A Jackson ally from Tennessee, he served as Speaker of the House of Representatives from 1835 to 1839 and later as governor of Tennessee. Polk had been angling for national office by advocating expansion in Texas and

> "a coward, a puppy, a liar, and a scoundrel generally"

Sold for Want of Use. Whig Henry Clay conducts an 1844 livestock auction of Democrats (the animals, from left to right, represent John Tyler, James K. Polk, and Martin Van Buren). *Source:* James S. Baillie and H. Bucholzer, *Sold for Want of Use.* United States, 1844. Courtesy of the Library of Congress, LC-USZ62-91407.

the Oregon Territory, and he came from relative obscurity to win the Democratic nomination (see figure 3.1).

Polk's leadership of the House of Representatives earned him the nickname "Polk, the plodder," but to supporters, he was "Young Hickory." Whig detractors such as Seargent Smith Prentiss considered him "a blighted burr that has fallen from the mane of the war-horse of the Hermitage." One newspaper even saw Polk's nomination as "the dying gasp, the last breath of life, of the 'Democratic' party."

However, Polk's Whig opponent, Henry Clay, had a long record in public life that worked against him. He was, according to one pamphlet, a "notorious Sabbath-breaker, Profane Swearer, Gambler, Common Drunkard, Perjurer, Duelist, Thief, Robber, Adulterer, Man-stealer, Slave-holder, and Murderer!" Polk narrowly defeated Clay in 1844 with some help from the Liberty Party candidate, who won over sixty thousand votes.

Polk had promised to serve a single term and stuck to that, but during his four years in office, over a million square miles of territory were added to the United States. John Tyler had gotten the controversial annexation of Texas approved in his last days in office, and Polk signed the agreement in December 1845. As new border disputes arose with Mexico, Polk launched the controversial Mexican-American War, lasting from April 1846 to February 1848. His dubious rationale prompted Abraham Lincoln, then a freshman member of the House, to call him "a bewildered, confounded, and miserably perplexed man." Lincoln also referred to Polk's justification for the war as "a half insane mumbling of a fever dream." Polk, in his 1846 message to Congress, characterized his critics as serving to "encourage the enemy" and "give them 'aid and comfort.'"

Polk

"a coward, a puppy, a liar, and a scoundrel generally"—former congressman Thomas Arnold in 1830, who put the insult in an ad in the *Knoxville Intelligencer*, attempting to provoke a duel. Polk ignored him. *Puppy* was an insulting term for a vain and conceited dandy.

"a cancer on the body politic"—Representative Henry Wise of Virginia, in 1834, when Polk was Speaker of the House. Wise also referred to Polk as a "petty tyrant." Chided for not responding to such taunts, Polk replied that he "had nothing to gain from street fighting, or low bullying gasconades."

"a coward, hiding behind his office to wage war against an unoffending neighbor"—Abraham Lincoln, introducing the Spot Resolutions in Congress, which called on Polk to identify the location of the supposed bloodshed used to justify the Mexican-American War.

"The Hangman of the Confederacy"—A Whig epithet used by opponents of the war.

a "robber-chief"—Thomas Corwin, a Whig senator from Ohio, addressing Polk in a speech in the Senate: "But you still say, you want room for your people. This has been the plea of every robber-chief from Nimrod to the present hour."

a knave—the *New York Herald* called Polk's statement that the United States held claim to the Oregon Territory "palpable knavery and babbling folly."

"mendacious"—Both Whigs and disaffected Democrats referred to Polk with this synonym for *dishonest*. Most notable is the speech of Senator Alexander Stephens in 1848, in which he explained, "Why, if a man were ambitious of acquiring a reputation for duplicity and equivocation, he could not select a better example in all history than to follow in the footsteps of our president. He did not know any better or more fitting appellation . . . than Polk the mendacious."

Old Rough and Ready (Zachary Taylor, 1849–1850)

As the 1848 election approached, the Whigs were searching for a candidate who could succeed in both the North and the South. Zachary Taylor fit the bill: a Louisiana plantation owner, a career military man, and popular war hero. Taylor had few stated positions, and the Whigs chose him as their nominee rather than take another chance with Henry Clay. Yet many were skeptical. Daniel Webster dismissed him as "an illiterate frontier colonel who hasn't voted in forty years," and a Democratic cartoon captioned "an Available candidate" showed a general, presumably Taylor, sitting atop a pile of skulls.

"a weak man made giddy with the idea of the presidency"

Taylor had been at odds with Polk, who fretted about the presidential aspirations of both Taylor and General Winfield Scott. Polk's diary refers to Taylor as lacking intellect and easily led. In one entry, Polk writes that Taylor "does not seem to have resources or grasp of mind enough" to command the army; in another he characterized him as a tool of "cunning and shrewd men of more talents than himself."

Taylor declared himself a Whig and ran as a man above politics, explicitly saying that he did not wish to be a party man. He defeated the general put up by the Democrats, Lewis Cass, as well as former president Van Buren (running on the Free Soil Party ticket).

During Taylor's short administration, he turned out to be more decisive than Polk had imagined. The extension or prohibition of slavery in the new territories was becoming ever more divisive, and in his 1849 message to Congress, Taylor proposed adding new states to the Union without resolving the issue of slavery in advance. He also came out against the Compromise of 1850, the suite of bills intended to address slavery in new territories, and when Southern politicians talked of leaving the Union, he privately threatened to hang secessionists. Taylor's administration lasted a short sixteen months, and the debate over the compromise shifted when he died after becoming sick following a Fourth of July celebration in 1850.

 SAID OF

Taylor

"a weak man . . . made giddy with the idea of the presidency . . . [H]e is a narrow-minded, bigoted partisan"— James K. Polk.

"wholly incompetent"—Henry Clay.

"a military autocrat"—An 1848 Democratic pamphlet called *A Northern No!* The pamphlet went on to compare Taylor to "Caesar and Cromwell."

"He passes away his life . . . in semi-stupefaction, and makes his understrappers do . . . all the work."—the Portland *Argus*.

"dilatory, temporizing, timorous"—the *Washington Union*, referring to Taylor's view on the Compromise of 1850.

lazy and unlearned—rival general Winfield Scott, who said that "few men ever had a more comfortable labor-saving contempt for learning of every kind."

unprepared—Whig Horace Greeley, the founding editor of the *New York Tribune*, who said, "Old Zack is a good old soul but doesn't know himself from a side of sole leather in ways of statesmanship."

"dead and gone to hell, and I am glad of it"—Brigham Young, then governor of the Utah Territory, who had been told that Taylor saw Mormons as "a pack of outlaws."

The American Louis Philippe
(Millard Fillmore, 1850–1853)

In July 1850, Vice President Millard Fillmore was sworn in as president. Though he grew up poor, Fillmore had an aristocratic manner, good looks, and polish, and he was called the "American Louis Philippe" (a reference to the French king). When Taylor was nominated in 1848, Fillmore was added to the ticket to appeal to Northerners.

> "he means well, but he is timid, irresolute, uncertain"

As president, Fillmore reversed Taylor's position and supported the Compromise of 1850, proposed by the aging Clay and shepherded to enactment by Stephen A. Douglas. As he struggled with the decision, Fillmore gained a reputation for indecisiveness. William H. Seward, a longtime New York rival, would write to his wife that "Providence has at last led the man of hesitation and double opinions to the crisis, where decision and singleness are indispensable." The *New York Daily Herald* noted his "dallying and indecision" and saw him as an "irresolute tranquil" man relying on "accomplishments of the past." Yet when Fillmore acted decisively, threatening to use force if Texas seized land from New Mexico, the *Austin Gazette* referred to his "despotic pretensions."

The Compromise of 1850 damaged Fillmore's re-election prospects. The eventual bill admitted California as a free state, created new territories of Utah and New Mexico, and ended the slave trade in Washington, D.C. But it also included the Fugitive Slave Act, which required officials and citizens in all states to co-operate in the return of escaped slaves. The compromise became unpopular both in the North, where abolitionists resisted enforcement of the Fugitive Slave Act, and in the South, where many opposed any restrictions on slavery. In 1852, the Whigs chose not to renominate the incumbent Fillmore.

 SAID OF

Fillmore

"a second-hand president"—Edward Moran, a White House attendant. A story of the time had it that Fillmore complained about the presidential carriage, asking, "How do you think it will do for the president of the United States to ride in a second-hand carriage?" and that Moran replied, "Sure, you know, excellency, you're only a second-hand president."

"a wife-made man"—Newspapers in 1850, referring to Abigail Fillmore's influence on her husband. She had been his teacher in the one-room schoolhouse he attended.

According to Horace Greeley, *"Fillmore lacks pluck. He wants backbone. He means well, but he is timid, irresolute, uncertain, and loves to lean."*

"cowardly"—the *New York Evening Post*, referring to Fillmore's "cowardly message in which he declared that Texas had a good title to New Mexico."

"a timid man"—the *Louisville Journal*, 1851.

"a small neighborhood candidate"—abolitionist editor Gamaliel Bailey, when Fillmore ran as the candidate of the anti-immigrant Know-Nothing Party in 1856.

"We loathe your dough-face, Fillmore"—line in an 1856 song promoting John C. Frémont.

Doughfaces and Copperheads

Damaged by the perception that the Compromise of 1850 favored the South, Millard Fillmore was characterized as a *doughface,* a term that would also be applied to Franklin Pierce and James Buchanan.

At the turn of the nineteenth century, a doughface was a fright mask made of wet flour; the *OED* cites its use from 1809 with this example: "It is something like dressing ourselves up in a dough-face and winding-sheet to frighten others." John Randolph used the term in a speech in Congress in 1833 to refer to Northern Democrats, who were "scared at their own dough-faces" and would fall in line with the South on slavery. By the 1850s, the term was widely used for Northern Democrats who sympathized with the South; the definition often was "a Northern man with Southern principles," though it was sometimes extended to Southern politicians opposed to slavery as well. John Russell Bartlett's *Dictionary of Americanisms* even cites a 1849 instance of the term *dough-facism*.

Copperhead was a term used to refer to the antiwar and proslavery Democrats of the Civil War era. The coinage by Republicans referred to the venomous snake and began to be used in print in 1861. (*Copperhead* had earlier been used to refer to the Dutch of New York and by some as a derogatory term for Native Americans.) Copperhead Democrats, in turn, tried to reframe the usage by treating the copper "head" as the likeness of Lady Liberty on the copper penny, which some even wore as badges. Copperheads inserted a peace plank in the 1864 Democratic Party platform, though it was repudiated by the party's candidate, General George McClelland.

The Hero of Many a Well-Fought Bottle
(Franklin Pierce, 1853–1857)

The tension between Northern abolitionists and Southern slaveholders grew violent during the presidential term of New

Englander Franklin Pierce, a Jacksonian Democrat. Son of a governor, Pierce served in the New Hampshire legislature and in both the House and the Senate. Polk, an old political ally, appointed him a brigadier general in the Mexican-American War. But Pierce had a drinking problem throughout his life, and a Whig slogan during the election of 1852 was that he was "the hero of many a well-fought bottle."

"a kind of third-rate county, or, at most, state politician"

Pierce had a doughface position on ending slavery; he wrote that it could only be abolished with the consent of Southerners or by force. That position, together with nominating convention rules favoring the South, enabled him to capture the Democratic nomination in 1852. He went on to narrowly defeat General Winfield Scott, the candidate of the fading Whig Party.

During Pierce's presidency, Senator Stephen Douglas proposed the Kansas-Nebraska Act, which allowed territories to decide the issue of slavery by vote. After Pierce signed the act into law, proslavery and antislavery forces flooded into Kansas, and fighting broke out in the towns of Lawrence and Pottawatomie. After the violence of "Bloody Kansas," abolitionist James Lane, who would later become one of Kansas's first senators, accused Pierce's administration of abetting murder.

By 1856, the Democrats had had enough of Pierce, the *New York Times* declaring him to be "a political Jonah," suggesting that "the only certainty is that Pierce will be thrown overboard." Democrats instead turned to James Buchanan, the minister to Britain. The Whigs were finished as a party, and the newly emergent Republicans nominated John C. Frémont. Pierce returned to New Hampshire and was a vocal critic of Abraham Lincoln during the Civil War, eventually dying of cirrhosis of the liver in 1869.

DANGEROUS CROOKED SCOUNDRELS

SAID OF

Pierce

"Fainting Frank"—a reference to the Battle of Contreras (1847), in which Pierce was thrown onto the pommel of his saddle and passed out.

"a dupe"—James Gordon Bennett of the *New York Herald*. A May 1856 report referred to Pierce's "follies, his imbecilities, his false promises, and still falser associates [which] have ruined him in his own party. He is merely a dupe in their hands."

"A New Hampshire, Democratic, doughface, militia colonel, a kind of third-rate county, or, at most, state politician"—Richard Henry Dana, later Lincoln's attorney general.

an "arch traitor"—Harriet Beecher Stowe. When Pierce's college friend Nathaniel Hawthorne planned to dedicate his novel *Our Old Home* to Pierce, Stowe wrote to Hawthorne's publisher, asking him to "tell me if our friend Hawthorne praises that arch-traitor Pierce in his preface and your loyal firm publishes it." Hawthorne toned down the dedication.

an imbecile—Ralph Waldo Emerson wrote in his journal that Pierce's "miserable administration admits but of one excuse, imbecility. Pierce was either the worst, or he was the weakest, of all our presidents."

"vain"—Gideon Welles, one of the founders of the Republican Party, wrote in 1868 that Pierce was "a vain, slow, and pliant man . . . [who] by his errors and weakness broke down his administration, and his party throughout the country."

"wholly without moral courage"—the *New York Herald*, in 1856.

a "black-hearted copperhead"—the *Hartford Courant*. Pierce's name figured prominently in anti-Copperhead posters, especially after an 1860 letter to Jefferson Davis was uncovered in which Pierce supported secession. Pierce was also accused of being part of the seditious Knights of the Golden Circle.

Old Buck (James Buchanan, 1857-1861)

James Buchanan made his fourth run for the presidency in 1856. Known by then as "Old Buck," he had served in the House and Senate and had also been secretary of state and minister to Russia. Seen by many as an experienced

> "a bloated mass of political putridity"

leader and peacemaker who might navigate the tense political climate, he emerged instead as an enabler of proslavery Southerners after the Supreme Court issued its *Dred Scott* decision denying citizenship rights to African Americans (*Dred Scott v. Sandford*, 1857) on the eve of his inauguration. Buchanan had many friends among Southern legislators and viewed abolitionists as dangerous agitators. His sympathies emboldened proslavery forces, especially when he endorsed a proslavery constitution in Kansas. By the time Buchanan left office, seven states had seceded while he vacillated. More would follow.

Buchanan's sexuality was often referred to disparagingly by contemporaries. He had a long-term relationship with Alabama senator William Rufus King, whom he met in 1821, and the two shared a room in a Washington boarding house for many years. Andrew Jackson called the pair "Aunt Fancy" and "Miss Nancy," using nineteenth-century slang. (The *OED* provides an 1824 citation to "Miss-nancy" as a reference to an effeminate man and an 1819 citation to *nancys* as a reference to buttocks.)

Others referred to them as "Siamese twins" and to King as "Buchanan's wife." Buchanan's and King's nieces later destroyed almost all of their correspondence. What little remains suggests a romantic relationship between the two, though that seems not to have hindered either Buchanan's or King's political careers. King was elected as Pierce's vice president, though he was too ill to serve, and he died of tuberculosis just forty-five days after being sworn in.

During his administration, Buchanan was vilified in the Northern press for corruption, for his conduct of foreign affairs, and as a "doughface" and "coward." By December 1860, the *Chicago Tribune* referred to him as "the chief of the traitors—the President of the United States." After he left office, Buchanan supported the Union and later attempted to defend himself in print in a memoir in which he blamed the war on Republican abolitionists. A review of the book in the *Christian Examiner* called Buchanan "the most amazing of fossils."

 SAID OF

Buchanan

"an inept busybody"—Andrew Jackson, referring to Buchanan's efforts in the 1824 election. Later as president, Jackson asked Buchanan to serve as minister to Russia, remarking that Russia "was as far as I could send him to get him out of my sights, and where he could do the least harm. I would have sent him to the North Pole if we had kept a minister there."

"Ten Cent Jimmy"—a Republican slogan from 1856, based on the claim that Buchanan would lower wages to ten cents a day.

"a bloated mass of political putridity"—Representative Thaddeus Stevens, a Radical Republican and fellow Pennsylvanian.

"a old dotard, an imbecile, a miserable gabbling old granny"—the *New York Herald* when Buchanan was running in 1856. He was sixty-five years old.

"our present granny executive"—Ulysses S. Grant, writing to a friend.

"that cowardly old imbecile & traitor Buchanan"—Senator George Gilman Fogg, writing to Lincoln in late 1860. Fogg added, "If ever hanging

were a proper use to put a man to for his political sins, he really deserves it."

"Judas"—Posters referred to Buchanan as "Judas." Printed envelopes showed his photo with JUDAS underneath and the description: "He was elected president by fraud and trickery! Under his administration the treasury was robbed! Duplicity and cowardice marked his career! Finally, he sold his country to a band of Southern conspirators."

"an old public functionary"—Buchanan referred to himself this way in his third State of the Union Address in 1859. The name was adopted by newspapers of the day, sometimes abbreviated as O.P.F.

"that pusillanimous dotard James Buchanan"—the *California Argus* in 1861.

From John Quincy Adams to James Buchanan, presidents were referred to as pimps and clowns, barbarians and monsters, villains and knaves, dotards, asses, accidents, and imbeciles, scoundrels and tyrants, dupes and doughfaces. The election of 1824 and the Jacksonian revolution of 1828 ushered in new voices and a taste for westward expansion. Sectionalism, growing moral realization, and a series of temporizing compromises and violent clashes brought the Union to the breaking point in 1860.

"Janus-faced"

FOUR

A Nation Remade, 1860–1900

When Abraham Lincoln was elected in 1860, seven states left the Union to form the Confederate States of America, and four more joined when hostilities began between the North and South. A bloody civil war lasted for over four years, with a staggering loss of more than six hundred thousand lives.

The postwar era was one of Republican dominance as the United States completed its westward expansion, industrialized, and began to assert itself internationally. Newspapers and magazines continued to grow in influence as their production became cheaper, leading to mass audiences for political commentary. Domestically, presidents struggled with civil rights issues and Reconstruction, immigration, the concentration of wealth, financial scandals, and civil service reform. Three of them were assassinated.

A Slang-Whanging Stump Speaker
(Abraham Lincoln, 1861–1865)

A self-educated lawyer with a sharp tongue, Abraham Lincoln made his way to the Illinois state legislature in the 1830s and 1840s and to the US House of Representatives in 1847 as a

"a third-rate Western lawyer"

Whig opponent of the war with Mexico. In 1858, Lincoln, by then a Republican, mounted an unsuccessful challenge to the sitting Democratic senator, Stephen Douglas, and set the stage for a run for the presidency in 1860.

Lincoln campaigned as an opponent of slavery, promising to limit its expansion into new territories. He won the Republican nomination on the third ballot, defeating frontrunner William H. Seward. Newspapers such as the *Albany Atlas and Argus*, supporting Seward, complained Lincoln was "charging for his speeches at the rate of one hundred dollars apiece," that he had never held "public office of any credit," and that he was "not known except as a slang-whanging stump speaker."

Other papers were harsher. The *New York Herald* referred to Lincoln as "a vulgar village politician" and "a third-rate Western lawyer" whose speeches were "unmitigated trash, interlarded with coarse and filthy jokes." The *Philadelphia Evening Journal* noted his "coarse language, his illiterate style, and his vulgar and vituperative personalities in debate."

In the general election campaign, Lincoln's looks were mocked. The *Houston Telegraph* described him as "hatchet-faced," adding, "He has most unwarrantably abused the privilege, which all politicians have, of being ugly." Newspapers in the South attacked Lincoln with racist cartoons, and the n-word was prominent, with papers and political opponents stoking fears of race-mixing, job replacement, and more.

Lincoln's chief opponent in the general election was once again Stephen Douglas, who led a fractured party. The Democrats experienced a walkout of Southern delegates and the formation of a separate Southern Democratic ticket led by

Buchanan's vice president, John C. Breckenridge (and endorsed by Tyler, Pierce, and Buchanan). Lincoln won decisively, with 180 electoral votes.

After Lincoln's election, representatives from seven Southern states met in Montgomery, Alabama, and established the Confederate States of America, with Jefferson Davis as president. When Confederate forces fired on Fort Sumter on April 12, 1861, the war began, and four more states joined the Confederacy.

Lincoln raised an army, declared martial law, expanded the powers of the executive, and issued the Emancipation Proclamation in January 1863, freeing the slaves in the Confederacy. His administration suspended habeas corpus and suppressed hundreds of newspapers. As the war progressed, Lincoln was often derided, and the Democrats won congressional majorities in 1862. General George McClellan, in letters to his wife, referred to Lincoln as "nothing more than a well-meaning baboon" and "the original gorilla." McClellan attributed the "original gorilla" characterization to Edwin Stanton, the secretary of war, who had also served as attorney general in the Buchanan administration.

In 1864 Lincoln won re-election, defeating McClellan, whom he had fired as commander of Union forces after the battle at Antietam. The war lasted until 1865; along the way, Lincoln instituted greenbacks (legal tender not backed by precious metals), conscription, and the nation's first income tax, all of which were controversial. Robert E. Lee surrendered at Appomattox on April 9, 1865, and five days later Lincoln was shot by John Wilkes Booth while attending a play at Ford's Theatre. He died the next day, April 15.

Lincoln

"a horrid-looking wretch"—the *Charleston Mercury*.

"wishy-washy"—the *Salem Advocate* in Lincoln's home state of Illinois, which opined: "His weak, wishy-washy, namby-pamby efforts, imbecile in matter, disgusting in manner, have made us the laughing stock of the whole world."

"illiterate"—Samuel F. B. Morse. The painter and telegraph inventor was a defender of slavery and a prominent Lincoln detractor, calling him "inhuman," "wicked," "irreligious," "without brains," and a "coarse, vulgar, uncultivated man."

"a barbarian"— George Templeton Strong, a prominent New York lawyer who kept a regular diary, referred to Lincoln as "a barbarian, Scythian, yahoo, or gorilla." Strong added, however, that Lincoln was "a most sensible straightforward, honest old codger."

"an idiot"—General George McClellan in a letter to his wife in 1861.

"a low, cunning clown"—attributed to Edwin Stanton by McClellan.

"Dishonest Abe"—disappointed abolitionist Elizabeth Cady Stanton, in a letter in 1864. Stanton said she would leave the country if Lincoln was re-elected.

"timid, vacillating & inefficient"—Republican senator Zachariah Chandler.

"an imbecile President"—the *Louisville Democrat*, after the Emancipation Proclamation, adding that the proclamation made Lincoln "an encourager of insurrection, lust, arson, and murder."

"this Presidential pigmy"—James Gordon Bennett, publisher of the *New York Herald*, commenting on Lincoln's renomination. Lincoln was six-foot-four, the tallest-ever president.

a *"half-witted Usurper who, in an evil hour, was elected . . . under the whip and spur of a set of fanatical and sectional politicians"*—Samuel Medary, editor of the *Crisis*, a Copperhead paper in Columbus, Ohio.

"a brainless tyrant"—the *Dubuque Herald*.

Stop the Presses

Abraham Lincoln had a complicated relationship with the press, which he relied on for news of the war and to carry reports of Union successes. But the press also sometimes revealed military secrets and objectives. Lincoln allowed the suppression or closing of more than three hundred newspapers. After trying persuasion, General George McClellan extended early-nineteenth-century articles of war by issuing orders that gave commanders authority over all correspondence and communication concerning the military.

The Copperhead Northern press was also brutally harsh to Lincoln, and in the summer of 1861, he denied the New York *Daily News* access to the postal system and had thousands of issues confiscated. As the war progressed, Lincoln's generals became more aggressive in jailing editors, threatening reporters, and closing newspapers. But public sentiment and legal opinion turned against press suppression, and Lincoln backed off.

Later wartime presidents relied on propaganda and censorship rather than outright suppression. Woodrow Wilson established the Committee of Public Information, which produced a daily bulletin of wartime propaganda and newsreels and introduced the character of Uncle Sam. However, the Espionage Act of 1917 and the Trading with the Enemy Act and the Sedition Act of 1918 gave the government broad power to suppress dissent, and thousands were arrested under the acts, including former presidential candidate Eugene V. Debs, convicted to a ten-year sentence for making an antiwar speech. And as wartime fears blended with the Red Scare that followed Russia's October Revolution in 1917, even more were arrested without warrants in the so-called Palmer Raids, named for Wilson's attorney general.

During World War II, Franklin Roosevelt established a wartime Office of Censorship by executive order in December 1941 and appointed the affable executive news editor of the Associated Press, Byron Price, as "Director of Censorship," overseeing a workforce that grew to 13,500 employees. When the *Chicago Tribune* revealed sensitive wartime information, FDR had his attorney general convene a grand jury investigation to determine if the newspaper had violated the Espionage Act. No indictment was returned.

Judas Johnson (Andrew Johnson, 1865–1869)

By 1864, Andrew Johnson had a thirty-year political career behind him, which included serving as governor of Tennessee and as a senator. A proslavery but also pro-Union Democrat, he was appointed by Lincoln as military governor of Tennessee after the war began and was added to the ticket when Lincoln ran for re-election.

"an insolent drunken brute"

His vice presidency had an inauspicious beginning. When he was inaugurated, Johnson appeared drunk—he had consumed several glasses of whiskey to fight a cold. His rambling, incoherent speech led the *New York World* to refer to him as "an insolent drunken brute in comparison with whom Caligula's horse was respectable." He became known as "Andy the sot," though Lincoln defended him when advisers asked about him, saying, "Andy ain't no drunk."

After Lincoln was killed, Johnson hurriedly instituted Reconstruction policies that blocked voting rights to blacks in the South, and he allowed Southern states to reinstitute de facto slavery under the so-called Black Codes. Johnson's approach put him at odds with Congress, which passed a series of civil rights laws over his veto and which passed the Fourteenth Amendment (adopted in 1868), establishing the principle of equal protection under the law for all citizens.

Unlike Lincoln, Johnson could not resist hitting back, and critics and *Harper's Weekly* would later cite his "intemperate, and often indecent, denunciation of his political opponents [which] reminds us of the demagogue rather than the well-balanced statesman." As early as July 1866,

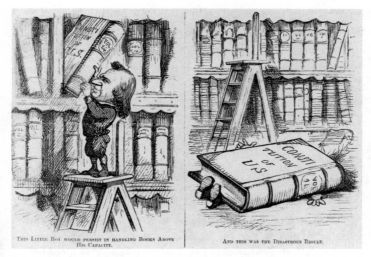

The Constitution takes down Andrew Johnson. "This little boy would persist in handling books above his capacity. And this was the disastrous result."
Source: Thomas Nast, *Harper's Weekly*, March 21, 1868. Courtesy of the Library of Congress, LC-USZ62-131563.

Horace Greeley's *New York Tribune* began calling him "Judas Johnson." In one fiery speech in St. Louis that fall, Johnson referred to that epithet, provoking a crowd of supporters to call for hanging his political opponents. Johnson answered with the rhetorical question, "Yes, why not hang them?" After the speech, the *Tribune* dubbed him "The Drunken Tailor," a reference to his occupation prior to entering politics, and the speech was later entered as evidence in his impeachment trial.

By 1867, some Republicans in Congress were even accusing Johnson of conspiring in the assassination of Lincoln. But the eventual legal basis of impeachment was Johnson's firing of War Secretary Edwin Stanton, in violation of the newly passed Tenure of Office Act intended to protect appointees. In February 1868, the House voted to impeach Johnson. He was acquitted in the Senate by a single vote.

 SAID OF

Andrew Johnson

"vindictive and perverse"—James K. Polk, in his *Diary*.

"this insolent, clownish creature"—the *New York World*.

"Whatever Andrew Johnson may be, he is no friend of our race"— Frederick Douglass, reporting on his observations on inauguration day. According to Douglass, Johnson glanced at him with "bitter contempt and aversion" and then assumed "the bland and sickly smile of the demagogue."

"If Andy Johnson was a snake, he would hide in the grass and bite the heels of rich men's children."—Tennessee governor Isham Harris.

"Andy, the bloody-minded tailor"—Mary Chesnut, in her Civil War diary.

"that renegade and traitor, Andrew Johnson"—A. J. Applegate, the Alabama lieutenant governor, in 1868, as Alabama was appointing senators to serve in the impeachment trial.

"an infernal liar"—Ulysses S. Grant.

an *"alien enemy, a citizen of a foreign state, and therefore not now legally President"*—Representative Thaddeus Stevens, presenting the impeachment charges in the Senate. The foreign state was the Confederacy.

"the great apostate," a *"faithless demagogue,"* the *"great accidental,"* the *"great pardoner"*—from circulars distributed by the *Cleveland Herald*, which hoped to see Benjamin Wade, president pro tem of the Senate,

installed in Johnson's place. A handful of Republicans voted against impeachment, in part to prevent Wade from assuming the presidency.

"demagogue and autocrat"—an *Atlantic Monthly* editorial of 1868,
which described Johnson as "insincere as well as stubborn, cunning as
well as unreasonable, vain as well as ill-tempered, greedy of popularity
as well as arbitrary in disposition, veering in his mind as well as fixed in
his will."

"the impersonation of the tyrannical slave power"—Senator Charles
Sumner, at the impeachment trial. At the time, *impersonation* could be
used to mean *personification*.

Useless Grant (Ulysses S. Grant, 1869–1877)

Ulysses S. Grant attended West Point, where
he excelled in horsemanship. In the 1840s, he
fought in the Mexican-American War, and he
served in the army until 1854. When the Civil
War began, Grant returned to duty, and his
discipline, knowledge of logistics, and aggres-

> "a man who
> has not an
> idea above a
> horse and a
> cigar"

siveness eventually brought him to command the main Northern
forces, which defeated Robert E. Lee's army in Virginia. In 1866,
Grant was named "general of the armies," the rank held by George
Washington.

Grant had broken with Andrew Johnson over Reconstruction
and was courted by Republicans, easily winning election
in 1868. In an interview with the *New York Herald* in 1869,
Johnson characterized Grant as "mendacious, cunning, and
treacherous" and as "nothing more than a bundle of petty spites,
jealousies, and resentments." Warming up, he added that Grant
was a "nonentity" with a soul "so small that you could put it
within the periphery of a hazel nutshell and it might float about

for a thousand years without knocking against the walls of the shell."

As president, Grant used the military to protect newly freed African Americans from groups like the Ku Klux Klan. However, he left much of the workings of the government to his cabinet and other appointees, so much so that the historian Henry Adams, John Quincy Adams's grandson, referred to Grant as a "baby politician," and one *Harper's* cartoon of the time showed a bearded baby Grant being cared for by Republican elders. Grant also appointed many friends to government positions, remaining loyal to them even when they were corrupt, and "Grantism" became a short-lived part of the American political vocabulary. Republican senator Charles Sumner coined the term in a long speech in 1872 titled "Republicanism vs. Grantism," in which he attacked the nepotism and corruption of Grant's administration, comparing it to the Roman Empire of Caesar. Sumner claimed that "the presidential office itself is treated as little more than a plaything. . . . [T]his exalted trust has dropped to be a personal indulgence, where palace cars, fast horses, and sea-side loiterings figure more than duties." Grant would later complain about the "fire of personal abuse, and slander" during his first term. In 1872, Grant faced a challenge from the so-called Liberal Republicans, who chose publisher Horace Greeley for the presidential race. Greeley was also nominated by the Democrats, who hoped to capitalize on Republican division. However, Grant was re-elected easily, and there were even higher Republican majorities in Congress.

Grant's second term included a depression, high unemployment, and further scandals involving members of his administration, though Grant himself remained a popular figure. After toying with a bid for a third term, Grant chose to retire, and in his final message to Congress he acknowledged that "mistakes have been made" in the selection of appointees but added that "no Administration from the time of Washington to the present has been free from these mistakes."

Soon in both financial and health trouble—throat cancer from smoking endless cigars—Grant died eight years after his term ended.

SAID OF
Grant

"Useless Grant"—a childhood nickname bestowed by other children. Grant's quietness was mistaken for stupidity.

"the Butcher"—the Democratic press, during the Civil War.

"a scientific Goth, resembling Alaric, destroying the country as he goes and delivering the people to starvation. Nor does he bury his dead, but leaves them to rot on the battlefield."—Major John Tyler, son of the former president, alluding to the sacking of Rome in 410 CE.

"surly"—The *Portsmouth Times*, a Democratic paper, had this to say in 1871 when Grant visited: "If Grant does look as though he had been drunk for a week, and act, in a surly, cold and indifferent manner toward the people who throng to see him, still it is wrong to treat him as other men should be treated for such conduct. Remember that he is president, and properly regard his high office."

"Grant the Drunkard"—headline in the *Akron Times* in 1872. The paper went on to advise: "When you are asked to vote for Grant, the drunkard, let the answer be a decided 'Never.'"

"uniquely stupid"—Henry Adams, sarcastically claiming that was what the initials "U.S." stood for. He added that "the progress of evolution from

President Washington to President Grant was alone enough to upset Darwin" and that Grant "should have lived in a cave and worn skins."

"a political ignoramus"—Gideon Welles, secretary of the navy under Lincoln and Andrew Johnson. Later Welles would refer to Grant as "a dangerous man . . . devoid of patriotism and principles."

"an ignorant soldier"—the *Nation*, in 1876, adding that Grant was "coarse in his taste and blunt in his perceptions, fond of money and material enjoyment and of low company."

"a man who has not an idea above a horse and a cigar"—Georgia Republican Joseph Emerson Brown.

"the great presidential quarreler, with more quarrels than all other Presidents together, all begun and continued by himself"—Senator Charles Sumner, in "Republicanism vs. Grantism."

"utterly indefensible in character, derogatory to the country and of evil influence"—Sumner.

"He had done more than any other president to degrade the character of cabinet officials. . . .His imperturbability is amazing. I am in doubt whether to call it greatness or stupidity."—James A. Garfield.

His Fraudulency (Rutherford B. Hayes, 1877–1881)

Rutherford Birchard Hayes was a criminal defense lawyer and Civil War colonel who served in Congress and was elected governor of Ohio.

"an amiable imbecile"

After losing a Senate bid in 1872, he retired from politics for a few years but came back to secure the Republican nomination in 1876, edging out frontrunner James G. Blaine. Facing off against the governor of New York, Samuel Tilden, Hayes lost the popular vote by about 250,000 votes. In the electoral college, Tilden garnered 184 electoral votes, one short of a majority, to Hayes's 165, but 20 votes were in dispute: 19 in the South and 1 in Oregon. A special commission established by Congress awarded those 20 votes and the presidency to Hayes.

Tilden would later predict that "this administration will be the greatest failure the Country ever saw," and the election prompted use of such terms as "His Fraudulency" and "The Pretender." Hayes's first name also lent itself to mockery, with political opponents calling him "Rutherfraud."

Hayes had hoped to be a uniter, and he extracted pledges from Democrats in the South to uphold civil rights. But when he removed the troops that were supporting Republican control of the region, the pledges were ignored.

Hayes also saw his role as a civil service reformer, and he skipped over the political lieutenants of party bosses for cabinet positions. One of his most implacable detractors was the powerful Republican senator Roscoe Conkling, who blocked his reform efforts and suggested that Hayes was a "usurper" with "a disturbed mind." Hayes responded that it was "useless to attempt to conciliate such a person" as Conkling.

Before being elected, Hayes had pledged not to seek re-election, and he honored that pledge, returning to Ohio and involving himself in a variety of progressive educational and social causes until his death in 1893.

SAID OF

Hayes

Henry Adams called Hayes *"a third-rate nonentity."* And Adams's wife, after meeting Hayes, opined that there was *"not a ray of force or intellect in forehead, eye or mouth."*

Justice Nathan Clifford, a dissenting member of the panel that gave Hayes the election, referred to him as *"the illegitimate president."*

"the bogus, fraudulent, so called President."—the *Greensboro Patriot*.

"a cheat"—Charles A. Dana, editor of the *Sun*, wrote of the election: "These are the days of humiliation, shame and mourning for every patriotic American. A man whom the people rejected at the polls has been declared President of the United States through processes of fraud. A cheat is to sit in the seat of George Washington."

"the weak and imbecile Hayes"—the *Millheim (PA) Journal*, in an 1877 piece called "The Finale: A Brief History of the Presidential Election."

Senator Roscoe Conkling commented in a speech: *"When Dr. Johnson defined patriotism as the last refuge of the scoundrel, he was unconscious of the then underdeveloped capabilities and uses of the word Reform."*

Conkling's supporters, the old guard or stalwart Republicans, referred to *"the old woman policy of Granny Hayes,"* a nickname that seems connected to Hayes's abstemious nature. Hayes was also purportedly known as *"Queen Victoria in breeches."*

Hayes is *"worse than a usurper. He is a weak and pliant tool of a set of men who do not propose to give up their hold on government until they destroy it. A fraud and a tool. Really, we are almost sorry for the Ohio weakling"*—editorial in the *Atlanta Constitution* in 1879.

"an amiable imbecile"—the *St. Louis Globe-Democrat* in 1881.

"one of the most unmitigated liars I ever knew"—Senator Zachariah Chandler of Michigan in 1882. He added that Hayes was "not only morally weak but he has no regard for the truth."

The Chief of the Conspirators (James A. Garfield, 1881)

Ohio's James A. Garfield served as president for just six and a half months. He was a legislator, clergyman, and soldier who made his way to the House of Representatives in 1863 as one of the so-called Radical Republicans, working his way up to the Republican leadership.

Garfield had served as a member of the electoral commission that awarded the 1876 election to Hayes, which later earned him the title "chief of the conspirators." In 1880, the Republicans were split. Grant was trying for a comeback, with the support of Roscoe Conkling. The other major contender was James G. Blaine, leader of the Half-Breed Republicans, so-called because they were open to civil service reform. Garfield was the convention manager of Ohio's senator John Sherman, who was running a distant third. As Sherman's hopes faded, the anyone-but-Grant forces coalesced around Garfield. Chester Arthur of New York, a Conkling supporter, was chosen as the vice presidential candidate. Garfield and Arthur went on to win the election by a narrow popular-vote margin.

The campaign was a rough one. Garfield was one of several congressmen who had accepted stock in Credit Mobilier, a railroad construction firm that had received loans and land grants from the government. Garfield had admitted that he had received $329 from the company (about $6,000 today), and the issue was revived in 1880.

Charles Dana of the *New York Sun* also revisited the Civil War firing of General William Rosecrans, publishing an account from Lincoln's postmaster general Montgomery Blair claiming that Garfield had denounced Rosecrans to Lincoln and Edwin Stanton. Blair called Garfield "a base fellow" and referred to Garfield's "betrayal" of Rosecrans. And in an October surprise, Tammany Hall's penny newspaper, the *Truth*, published a letter supposedly from Garfield that endorsed unlimited Chinese immigration. When

Garfield demonstrated that the letter was forged, opposition papers dubbed him a liar.

As president, with Blaine as his secretary of state, Garfield battled his own party's leaders over federal appointments and, like Hayes, angered Conkling. Conkling referred to Garfield's appointments as "perfidy without parallel," and Grant broke off relations with Garfield as well. Vice President Chester Arthur criticized him in the press. It was not an auspicious beginning.

On the second of July 1881, Garfield was shot in the back twice by Charles Guiteau, a lawyer whose many applications for a federal job had been rejected. Incapacitated, Garfield survived through the summer until September 19, when he died of complications from the shooting.

 SAID OF

Garfield

"the ready champion of rings and monopolies"—an 1876 resolution by Warren County, Ohio, Republicans.

"an angleworm"—Senator Roscoe Conkling.

lacking *"the backbone of an angleworm"*—Ulysses S. Grant in 1881.

"a clever trickster" who had made a *"hypocritical pretense of supporting Sherman"*—the *Concord (NH) People and Patriot.*

a *"perjurer"*—the 1880 *Democratic Campaign Handbook*, referring to Garfield's testimony in the Credit Mobilier case.

"his character is as dubious as his talents are unquestioned."—Joseph Pulitzer's *St. Louis Post-Dispatch.*

"Janus-faced"—the *Democratic Campaign Handbook*, referring to Garfield's position on Chinese immigration.

"not only a liar, but a false swearer and a bribe-taker"—the *Boston Globe*, in October 1880.

"nothing more than a big, confused Newfoundland dog"—a sympathetic politician during Garfield's tenure.

"our president-czar"—the *National Republican*, in early May 1881. Tsar Alexander II had been assassinated in March of that year. The article also compared Garfield to Napoleon and Charles I of England.

"Garfield has not been square, nor honorable, nor truthful"—Chester Arthur, Garfield's vice president, speaking to the editor of the *New York Herald*.

The Gentleman Boss (Chester A. Arthur, 1881–1885)

Chester Arthur began his career as a New York lawyer and served as the quartermaster general for New York during the Civil War. Arthur was a supporter of party boss Roscoe Conkling, who arranged for him to be appointed collector of the Port of New York in 1871, a position re-

> "the stalled ox feeding at the rich trough of accident"

sponsible for kickbacks to the party coffers. His reputation as a high-rolling machine politician earned him the nickname "The Gentleman Boss." Civil service reformer Silas Burt, a longtime friend of Arthur's, referred to him as outwardly "bland and accommodating," but "the leader of a corps of partisan mercenaries" and a member of a party that had become "a mere stalking horse for as corrupt a band of varlets as ever robbed a public treasury."

In 1877, Arthur lost his job at the Port of New York. After a commission appointed by President Rutherford B. Hayes documented patronage and kickbacks, Hayes issued an executive order prohibiting the practice. Arthur ignored the order, so Hayes fired him. Arthur remained an influential New York politician, however, and was nominated as the vice presidential candidate in 1880 to appease Conkling's supporters. Social reformer Charles Eliot Norton referred to Arthur's nomination as "a miserable farce," and the *New York Times* called Arthur "about the last man who would be considered eligible" for the presidency.

Arthur played an important role in the 1880 campaign, but he and James Garfield were never close, and during Garfield's brief administration, the two were at odds over appointments, as Garfield sought to reduce Conkling's power. It seemed that Arthur would forever be "Conkling's man Friday," as the *St. Louis Post-Dispatch* called him.

Yet when he assumed the presidency after Garfield's assassination, Arthur distanced himself from Conkling and supported the Pendleton Act of 1883, which prohibited kickbacks and instituted competitive exams for civil service positions. Arthur found himself disagreeing with Republican leaders on other issues as well, such as tariffs, and in 1884, both Conkling and former president Grant opposed his renomination. The nomination instead went to James Blaine on the fourth ballot. Unknown to most of the public, Arthur was suffering from a fatal kidney ailment, Bright's disease, which had been diagnosed in 1882. He died in 1886.

 SAID OF

Arthur

"a coward and an ingrate"—Charles Guiteau, Garfield's assassin, in his final statement. Guiteau added: "His ingratitude to the man that made him and saved his party and land from overthrow, has no parallel in history." Guiteau was hanged in 1882.

DANGEROUS CROOKED SCOUNDRELS

"better fitted to be a scullion at Delmonico's [restaurant] than in the White House"—John Jarrett, president of the Amalgamated Iron and Steel Workers.

"the stalled ox feeding at the rich trough of accident"—former senator Stephen Dorsey, who was prosecuted in 1882 and 1883 when the Star Route Scandal came to light.

not an American—In 1880 Democrats challenged Arthur to produce proof of his citizenship and hired an investigator to research Arthur's past. Arthur ignored the claims, but the investigator later published them in a book titled *How a British Subject Became the President of the United States.*

"not broad enough in mental equipment"—the *New York Tribune*, in Arthur's obituary.

a "flathead"—Mark Twain, using the slang of the time for a simpleton. Speaking at a Republican meeting in Hartford, Connecticut, in 1876, Twain was bemoaning patronage: "But when you come to our civil service," he said, "we serenely fill great numbers of our minor public offices with ignoramuses; we put the vast business of a custom house in the hands of a flathead who does not know a bill of lading from a transit of Venus, never having heard of either of them before." Twain later revised his opinion of Arthur.

ETYMOLOGICAL EXPLORATIONS

Flatheads, Imbeciles, and Idiots

Mark Twain referred to Chester Arthur as a *flathead*, a term for a fool or simpleton. Twain also invoked the word in *The Adventures of Huckleberry Finn*, when the king and the duke bilk some "Greenhorns [and] flatheads." The term seems to have not made much headway in general use, perhaps because of competition with other uses of *flathead* or from competition with *fathead*, which was emerging in the nineteenth century as well. *Blockhead*, incidentally, goes back to the 1500s, and the device of compounding *head* with a derisive term was already well established by the nineteenth century.

The most common nineteenth-century way of mocking a president's intelligence seems to have been to use *imbecile*, a word borrowed into English from French. Tyler, Pierce, Buchanan, Lincoln, and others were all characterized that way. *Imbecile* previously had the meaning of feeble or physically weak. By the eighteenth century, it had come to apply to the mind as well, and Johnson's 1755 *Dictionary of the English Language* gave the definition as "weak; feeble; wanting strength of either mind or body." By the nineteenth century, the sense of mental deficiency was ascendant, and *imbecile* could be used either as an adjective or a noun.

Lincoln was also called an *idiot*, another word borrowed from French (perhaps even earlier than *imbecile*). It originally simply meant a person without learning—someone who was a layperson and unlettered. Over the course of the fifteenth century, *idiot* came to denote a person with a condition of "profound mental disability" as well as someone "who speaks or acts in what the speaker considers an irrational way, or with extreme stupidity or foolishness." And for a time, *idiot* was also a synonym for *court jester*.

British law adapted *idiot* as a technical term for *developmental disability* as early as 1600, and for a time in the early twentieth century, *idiot* and *imbecile* were repurposed as part of the clinical vocabulary of psychology, notably in Edmund Blake Huey's 1912 book *Backward and Feeble-Minded Children*. Huey added the term *moron*, a twentieth-century neologism coined from the Greek word meaning *foolish* (and thus cognate with *sophomoric*).

Today the clinical use of *idiot*, *imbecile*, and *moron* is considered outdated and offensive.

The Stuffed Prophet
(Grover Cleveland, 1885–1889 and 1893–1897)

Grover Cleveland's political career began with a run for mayor of Buffalo, New York, in 1881. He rose quickly as an anticorruption politician, so quickly in fact that he was elected governor in 1882 and won the Democratic nomination for the presidency in 1884. Cleveland narrowly

"a man stained with disgusting infamy"

DANGEROUS CROOKED SCOUNDRELS

defeated former secretary of state James G. Blaine, who was abandoned by reformist Republican Mugwumps. It was a contentious election, with candidates from the Greenback Party, the Prohibition Party, the Equal Rights Party, and more. Character was an issue for both major-party candidates. Blaine had a reputation for influence peddling and public corruption. Cleveland had seduced a widow and fathered an illegitimate child. The *New York Sun* and the *New York Tribune* offered these characterizations of Cleveland when the story of the son he had with Maria Halpin became news: he was a "rake," a "libertine," the "father of a bastard," "a gross and licentious man," a "moral leper," and "a man stained with disgusting infamy." The *Sun* also referred to the 250-pound Cleveland as "The Stuffed Prophet." In the end, the voters cared less about sex than about corruption, and Cleveland was elected.

As president, Cleveland initiated little legislation but used the veto extensively. He opposed the prohibition of alcohol but was silent on the emerging issue of women's rights and sided with Southern Democrats on race. He did court new immigrant voters and took aggressive positions with respect to US regional hegemony, in one instance even threatening war with Britain.

Cleveland was thin-skinned about criticism, keeping the press at a distance and often writing answers to publications that criticized him. At one point, he responded to a satire in the humor magazine *Puck* with a letter exclaiming, "I don't think that there ever was a time when newspaper lying was so general and so mean as at present."

Cleveland's two terms as president were interrupted by the presidency of Benjamin Harrison. During Cleveland's second term, the economy suffered from the worst depression to that time, with 18 percent unemployment. Cleveland attempted to solve the crisis by repealing the Silver Purchasing Act of 1890, which required the coinage of silver but depressed the price of gold. The action split his own party. By 1896, he faced a rebellion from populist Democrats, and the 1896 party candidate, William Jennings Bryan, accused him of infecting the party with a "Republican virus." Cleveland did not support Bryan in the election, writing that Bryan "has not the remotest notion of the principles of Democracy."

 SAID OF

Cleveland

debauched—Charles Dana of the *New York Sun*, a one-time Cleveland supporter, called him "a coarse debauchee who would bring his harlots with him to Washington and hire lodgings for them convenient to the White House." Dana also referred to Cleveland's "plodding mind, limited knowledge, and narrow capacities."

"an artful seducer, a foe to virtue, an enemy of the family"—Reverend George Ball of Buffalo, on the Halpin affair.

a "besotted tyrant"—Democratic senator Ben Tillman called Cleveland that in 1896, adding that he was "self-idolatrous . . . an arrogant and obstinate ruler." Tillman promised to stick a pitchfork into Cleveland's "fat ribs," leading to his being called "Pitchfork Ben."

"a damned traitor, that's what he is"—Democratic congressman H. L. Snodgrass in 1896. Snodgrass was referring to Cleveland's position against the coinage of silver.

a "puppet of the gold bugs of Wall Street"—an 1892 editorial in the Kearney, Nebraska, *Daily Hub*, endorsing Benjamin Harrison.

"To laud Clevelandism on Jefferson's birthday is to sing a Te Deum in honor of Judas Iscariot on a Christmas morning!"—Democratic governor John Altgeld of Illinois at a Jefferson Day celebration.

"a bunko steerer"—William Jennings Bryan, using a then-common term for con man.

"The Fat Incubus"—headline in the *New York Sun* in 1891.

"the agent of Jewish bankers and British gold"—Mary Elizabeth Lease, the anti-Semitic populist who advised farmers to "raise less corn and more hell." She also called Cleveland "a fat old bull."

The Human Iceberg (Benjamin Harrison, 1889–1893)

Benjamin Harrison served as a brigadier general in the Civil War and, following a family tradition, became involved in politics. He was the grandson of William Henry Harrison and the great-grandson of a signer of the Declaration of Independence, after whom he was named.

> "a stinking little aristocrat"

After the Civil War, Harrison made an unsuccessful run for the Indiana governorship in 1876. In 1880, he was elected to the US Senate. In 1888, Harrison was a dark-horse candidate for the Republican nomination but won it on the eighth ballot, over Ohio's John Sherman and several others. Harrison went on to defeat Cleveland in the electoral college, 233 to 168, despite losing the popular vote; Cleveland's New York and Harrison's Indiana had flipped to the Republicans.

Born into relative privilege, Harrison was confident in his abilities but bookish and formal, so much so that his staff called him "the human iceberg," and Harrison often found himself apologizing for his brusque behavior. As president, Harrison supported protective tariffs along with the Sherman Silver Purchase Act. Democrats retook control of Congress in 1890, and Harrison eventually lost support in his own party over cabinet appointments. The public saw Harrison as out of touch on economic issues.

His relationship with his secretary of state, James G. Blaine, was also an issue as the 1892 election approached, and the two were barely on speaking terms toward the end of the administration. When Blaine resigned a few days before the Republican Convention of 1892, he was put forward as a candidate in competition with Harrison, as was William McKinley. One newspaper suggested that Republican politicians "could no longer endure Harrison's cold-blooded and despotic sway," and Blaine was said to be "a victim of Harrison's frigidity, jealousy and ingratitude." Cleveland made a decisive comeback in 1892, again flipping New York and Indiana, and winning Illinois and Wisconsin as well.

 SAID OF

Benjamin Harrison

"Little Ben"—Harrison was nicknamed for his height (five-foot-six). He was also derisively known as "Grandfather's Hat" after his campaign slogan, "Grandfather's Hat Fits Ben," which suggested the presidency was in his lineage.

"a stinking little aristocrat [who] never recognized men on the street"—characterization of Harrison by Republican detractors in the gubernatorial contest of 1872.

"Kid Glove Harrison"—another nickname, referring to Harrison's wearing of goat-skin gloves. Democrats used it to reinforce Harrison's aristocratic image.

"the everlasting friend of monopoly and the foe of the workingmen"—Eugene V. Debs.

"the refrigerator"—Republican national chairman James Clarkson, a reference to Harrison's coldness.

"narrow, unresponsive, and oh so cold"—Walter Wellman of the *Chicago Tribune*. Wellman also quoted an anonymous senator as commenting

DANGEROUS CROOKED SCOUNDRELS

that having a conversation with Harrison was "like talking to a hitching post."

"cold-blooded, selfish, and grasping"—the *Vicksburg Evening Post*, complaining about Harrison's appointment of an African American as postmaster of Vicksburg, Mississippi.

"grouchy"—Ohio governor Joseph Foraker, in a 1916 memoir.

"as glacial as a Siberian stripped of his furs"—Senator Thomas Platt, who also called Harrison the "White House iceberg" and described him as a "pouter pigeon." Platt had been passed over for treasury secretary.

"that obstinate and pugnacious little President"—British minister Julian Pauncefote, who was negotiating with Harrison over seal-hunting issues.

"a cold-blooded, narrow-minded, prejudiced, obstinate, timid old psalm-singing Indianapolis politician"—the young Theodore Roosevelt.

"the little gray man in the White House"—Roosevelt again, who said that Harrison treated him "with cold and hesitating disapproval."

A Sad Jellyfish (William McKinley, 1897–1901)

A protégé of Rutherford B. Hayes, William McKinley represented Ohio in Congress and served as its governor from 1892 to 1896. Heavily funded by supporter Mark Hanna, McKinley defeated the populist William Jennings Bryan, who gave his famous "Cross of Gold Speech" at the Democratic National Convention in Chicago advocating the coinage of silver to increase the money supply. McKinley supported the gold standard.

"destined for a statue in a park, and practicing the pose for it"

As president, McKinley led the United States into the Spanish-American War in 1898. Through 1897, McKinley and many in the business community had hoped to resolve issues surrounding the Cuban independence movement peacefully, but public opinion, shaped by the newspapers of Hearst and Pulitzer, pushed politicians to war. In 1898, two months after the sinking of the USS *Maine* in Havana harbor, the ten-week war began. It resulted in the United States taking control of former Spanish colonies in the Philippines, Puerto Rico, and Guam, and in protectorate status for the newly independent Cuba.

McKinley was deft at handling criticism and political attacks, ignoring the many cartoons and comments published about him. He could, on occasion, respond high-mindedly, as he did when the nativist American Protective Organization spread rumors that candidate McKinley was secretly Catholic and had discriminated against Protestants in appointments. McKinley turned the tables, accusing them of being "the leaders of a secret order seeking . . . to dictate a presidential nomination."

McKinley was renominated in 1900, with the young Theodore Roosevelt as his running mate. Facing Bryan again, McKinley easily won re-election, bringing along even bigger Republican majorities in Congress. In the fall of 1901, tragedy struck while McKinley was visiting the Pan-American Exposition in Buffalo, New York. Shaking hands that afternoon at a reception at the Temple of Music, McKinley was shot twice in the chest by a young anarchist named Leon Czolgosz. McKinley died eight days later, and Theodore Roosevelt was sworn in as president.

 SAID OF

McKinley

"weak and a bidder for the admirations of the crowd"—from a letter written by the Spanish minister to the United States, revealed in William

DANGEROUS CROOKED SCOUNDRELS

Randolph Hearst's *New York Journal*. Less than a week later, an explosion destroyed the *Maine*.

"a white-livered cur"—Teddy Roosevelt, assistant secretary of the navy, when McKinley did not declare war immediately after the destruction of the *Maine*. He added that "the President has no more backbone than a chocolate éclair."

"Mr. Face-both-ways"—Andrew Carnegie, in a letter to Secretary of State John Hay. Carnegie was an officer in the Anti-Imperialist League, which had been formed in 1898 to oppose the American annexation of the Philippines. Carnegie also referred to McKinley as behaving like a "jellyfish," concealing itself with "ebullitions of blubber."

"a man of jelly, who would turn us all loose to the mob and not say a word"—African American journalist T. Thomas Fortune, on McKinley's civil rights policies.

"He was destined for a statue in a park, and was practicing the pose for it."—journalist William Allen White.

"the most hated creature on the American continent"—Arthur Brisbane, the editor of Hearst's *New York Journal*, in an editorial.

"a dangerous set of scoundrels"—E. L. Godkin of the *Nation*, describing McKinley and his cabinet.

"a sad jellyfish"—Henry Adams.

"a piece of affable putty"—writer Julian Hawthorne, son of Nathaniel.

"the Ohio twaddler"—journalist Frank Sanborn.

McKinley *"kept his ear so close to the ground, it was full of grasshoppers"*— Representative Joseph Cannon, referring to McKinley's tendency to follow public opinion.

"president of the money kings and trust magnates"—anarchist Emma Goldman. She also compared Czolgosz to Marcus Brutus.

Mark Hanna's *"echo, his slave, his suit of clothes"*—poet Vachel Lindsay.

"the enemy of the good people—the good working people"—assassin Leon Czolgosz.

"Thimblerigger"

FIVE

The Modern Presidency, 1900–1945

The period from 1900 to 1945 saw further changes to the nation and to the presidency. Philosophies of activism and social reform alternated with those of individualism and limited government. Prohibition (1920–1933) came and went. New technologies such as cars, movies, and radio took hold, along with new forms of culture such as jazz, film, and advertising. Women gained the right to vote in 1920. The economy entered a period of speculative growth followed by a devastating collapse, which left nearly a quarter of the workforce unemployed. And the United States overcame its isolationism, taking a decisive role in two world wars and helping to reshape the international order.

The new era began in September 1901.

That Damned Cowboy (Theodore Roosevelt, 1901–1909)

Theodore Roosevelt grew up as an asthmatic son of wealthy parents in New York City. Equally committed to physical and intellectual exercise, Teddy studied at Harvard and, after a flirtation with law school, entered the New York Assembly in 1882, at the age of twenty-four. When his

"utterly without conscience and regard for the truth"

young wife died, he took a two-year sabbatical to the Dakota Badlands. After his return, he continued his political and literary careers, winning appointment to the US Civil Service Commission and becoming president of the New York City Police Board and then assistant secretary of the navy.

During the Spanish-American War, Roosevelt commanded the volunteer cavalry unit called the Rough Riders and became known as the hero of San Juan Hill. The New York governorship followed, and when McKinley's first vice president died in office, Roosevelt was put on the national ticket in 1900—in part at the behest of New York political bosses, who did not want him to run for a second term as governor. Powerbroker and McKinley ally Mark Hanna called Roosevelt "that damned cowboy"; at the 1900 nominating convention, Hanna reportedly noted that "there's only one life between this madman and the Presidency."

As president, Teddy Roosevelt pursued an activist, progressive agenda and frightened the business community with his application of the Sherman Anti-Trust Act of 1890 and his intervention in labor issues. Yet he mended fences with conservative Republicans and business donors sufficiently to easily gain election to a full term in 1904.

Roosevelt used executive orders to create 150 new national forests and supported national consumer standards in the meatpacking and other industries. He also extended the globalist foreign policy path set by his most recent predecessors. In the case of the Panama Canal, his efforts included supporting a revolution and establishing Panama as a US protectorate.

Roosevelt considered himself a man of action and a fighter, and he bristled at criticism. Writer Henry James referred to him as "a dangerous and ominous jingo." The word, adapted from the earlier exclamation "By Jingo!," was at that time used as a noun for a blustering militarist. Roosevelt shot back that James was a "little emasculated mass of inanities." At the end of his presidency, after Pulitzer's *New York World* had published what he considered "a string of infamous libels," Roosevelt threatened to have Pulitzer prosecuted. When the Supreme Court decided in favor of Pulitzer's *World* in 1909, the paper gloated: "The decision is so sweeping that no other President will be tempted to follow in the footsteps of Theodore Roosevelt, no matter how greedy he may be for power, no matter how resentful of opposition."

 SAID OF

Theodore Roosevelt

"Jane-Dandy"—Comments in the press after Roosevelt's 1882 debut in the New York Assembly. The papers also referred to him as "our own Oscar Wilde," "the exquisite Mr. Roosevelt," and "the chief of the dudes." Roosevelt's later-adopted cowboy persona enabled him to shake that image.

"the mere monstrous embodiment of unprecedented and resounding Noise"—Henry James.

"utterly without conscience and regard for the truth, the greatest fakir of all times."—Warren Harding during the 1912 election.

a *"pirate,"* *"deliberately misleading the public"*—Congressman Frank Mondell, when Roosevelt accused Taft of cheating in the renomination process.

a *"drunk"*—George A. Newett, a Marquette, Michigan, newsman called Roosevelt that in 1913. Roosevelt sued for libel, won, and asked for six cents in damages.

the *"servile functionary of the trusts"*—socialist Eugene V. Debs.

"the bell hop of Wall Street"—progressive reformer Amos Pinchot in 1916.

"clearly insane"—Mark Twain. Twain also considered him "the most formidable disaster that has befallen the country since the Civil War."

a *"demagogue and a flatterer"*—William Howard Taft. By 1912, Roosevelt was running against his former protégé as a third-party candidate. Taft also called him a "dangerous egotist," a "freak," and a "honeyfuggler," a term for a swindler or flatterer.

a *"thimblerigger plying his vocation among the rural visitors to the midway plaisance"*—the Washington *Times* in 1912. A *thimblerigger* was a con man whose trade was the shell game.

"a charlatan of the highest skill"—*Baltimore Sun* columnist H. L. Mencken, who also referred to Roosevelt using the now obsolete synonym "mountebank." To Mencken, Roosevelt was "a quite typical member of the upper bourgeoisie. . . . Blatant, crude, overly confidential, devious, tyrannical, vainglorious, sometimes quite childish."

Smiling Bill (William Howard Taft, 1909–1913)

Born into a prominent Republican family in Ohio, William Howard Taft worked in a variety of legal and judicial positions, eventually rising to be solicitor general and a member of the US Court of Appeals. Taft seemed destined for a position on the Supreme Court, but William McKinley instead appointed him to the commis-

"he no doubt means well, but he means well feebly"

sion governing the Philippines. Roosevelt later made him the first civilian governor of the territory and then appointed Taft his secretary of war, a position Taft's father had held in the Grant administration.

Known as "Smiling Bill," the affable Taft became Roosevelt's confidant and chosen successor, and he defeated the

Taft caught napping by Teddy. Taft has become entangled in yarn, representing the legislative and financial issues of his administration. *Source:* Udo J. Keppler, "Goodness gracious! I must have been dozing!," June 22, 1910. Courtesy of the Library of Congress, LC-DIG-ppmsca-27643.

by-now-perennial candidate William Jennings Bryan. As president, Taft reined in many of Roosevelt's progressive initiatives and rejected the former president's New Nationalism.

By 1912, Taft and Roosevelt were bitterly opposed, and Roosevelt ran against Taft in the new system of presidential primary elections. He entered the 1912 Republican Convention with 271 pledged delegates to Taft's 71. Taft, however, had the support of the party bosses and won the nomination. Roosevelt continued to run as the candidate of the new Progressive Party, but the split among the Republicans handed the election to the Democrats, breaking a dozen years of Republican control.

Taft was appointed chief justice of the Supreme Court in 1921, serving until a month before his death in 1930. The other justices called the 350-pound Taft "Big Chief."

💬 SAID OF

Taft

"Taft is a blunderer. . . . He is too small for the position he aspires to"—an editorial in the Columbus, Kansas, *Modern Light*.

"A fathead"—Teddy Roosevelt. By 1912, Roosevelt no longer saw Taft as "Smiling Bill." Instead Teddy referred to him as a "man with brains of about three guinea-pig power," a "puzzlewit," and a "flubdub with a streak of the second-rate and the common in him."

"the golf pig"—the writer, nun, and social worker Rose Hawthorne Lathrop, known as Mother Mary Alphonsa.

"Mr. Malaprop"—Taft's political errors led to this nickname (Harding was yet to come), and Taft was also called "the Van Buren of his party."

"simply big, fat, and lazy"—Norman Hapgood, editor of *Collier's* magazine.

"He no doubt means well, but he means well feebly"—Teddy Roosevelt.

"just an easy-going fat man"—Robert LaFollette.

"the blundering politician, the honest greenhorn at the poker table"—journalist Charles Thompson, author of *Presidents I've Known and Two Near Presidents*.

A Trained Elocutionist (Woodrow Wilson, 1913–1921)

Woodrow Wilson was the son of a Presbyterian minister and his English wife, born and raised in the South. He attended the College of New Jersey and completed a PhD in history and political science at Johns Hopkins University in 1886. In 1902, he returned to his alma mater (now renamed Princeton University) as its president. From there, he became governor of New Jersey in 1910 and a Democratic candidate for the presidency in 1912.

> "neither a gentleman nor a real man"

Wilson faced Republicans divided between Roosevelt and Taft, and he won a decisive victory with his New Freedom platform. As president, Wilson replaced high tariffs with a graduated income tax, reshaped the banking system by instituting the Federal Reserve, established new agencies for consumer protection and safety, continued the attack on monopolies, and supported progressive measures in all areas but race, where he allowed federal segregation to be expanded in the civil service.

During his presidency, Wilson was derided as both a "dictator" and a "coward," many of the comments coming from Roosevelt and other Republicans. Personally aloof, Wilson rarely responded publicly to criticism, though he scolded the Associated Press editors when he addressed them in 1915 for letting "the rumors of irresponsible persons and origins get into the atmosphere of the United States." Wilson was referring to Roosevelt's criticism of his caution after the sinking of the *Lusitania*.

Narrowly re-elected in 1916 on the slogan "He Kept Us Out of War," Wilson led the nation into the global conflict in 1917 after secret German overtures to Mexico were revealed. In 1917 and 1918, Wilson also signed the new Espionage and Sedition Acts, under which about fifteen hundred people were arrested in the nation's first Red Scare in 1918 and 1919. After World War I (1914–1917), Wilson proposed a League of Nations and a new international order. While on a national tour to build support for the League, he suffered a stroke on September 25, 1919, which left him partially paralyzed and nearly blind. He spent the remainder of his term in seclusion and died three years after leaving office.

SAID OF

Wilson

"dishonorable"—Princeton trustee Grover Cleveland, when Wilson was president of that university.

"a liar and an ingrate"—New Jersey political boss Jim Nugent, when Wilson was governor.

prejudiced—The *New York Age*, an African American newspaper, said that Wilson had "most of the prejudices of the narrowest type of southern white." Wilson's resegregation of the federal workforce ended years of progress under previous presidents.

"the devil"—Henry Watterson, publisher of the Louisville *Courier-Journal*, said, "In any contest of three tickets headed respectively by Taft, Roosevelt and the devil, the *Courier-Journal* would . . . be obliged to support his satanic majesty." He was alluding to Wilson.

"usurper or dictator"—Senator Lawrence Sherman of Illinois, criticizing the League of Nations proposal (which he called "a Pandora's box full of evil"). Sherman also referred to Wilson as "our Caesar."

When Wilson failed to act after a German torpedo struck the *Lusitania*, killing 128 Americans, he (like Benjamin Harrison) was criticized as *"a human icicle."* The name stuck, and when Wilson visited California in 1919, the *San Diego Union* wrote, *"Folks say—some folks say—that Woodrow Wilson is a human icicle."* Wilson's 1916 opponent, Charles Evans Hughes, also had a reputation for coldness. He was referred to as "the bearded icicle."

Teddy Roosevelt called Wilson a *"prime jackass"* and a *"coward,"* adding that he would *"skin him alive if he doesn't go to war."*

"effeminate"—Henry Estabrook, a Republican hopeful in 1916, who said, "Mr. Wilson is by nature effeminate. He is robust only in words and even those have more fat than fibre, beautiful in contour but lacking in muscle."

"To call Mr. Wilson a weathercock is unfair to weathercocks." —Estabrook.

H. L. Mencken described Wilson's rhetoric as *"the idiotic babbling of a Presbyterian evangelist turned prophet and seer."*

"a strutting pedagogue" and an *"unctuous charlatan"*—writer Julian Hawthorne.

More from Teddy Roosevelt: Wilson was *"a less virile me," "yellow all through," "a trained elocutionist,"* and *"neither a gentleman nor a real man."*

"incompetent"—John Maynard Keynes, one of the British delegates at the Versailles Conference, said, "There can seldom have been a statesman of the first rank more incompetent in the agilities of the council chamber."

ETYMOLOGICAL EXPLORATIONS

Yellow Streak

In 1916, the *Chicago Tribune* editorialized that Woodrow Wilson was turning the United States into a "yellow" nation and that a vote for Wilson was a vote for cowardice. The paper wrote, "Europe already thinks the United States is yellow. Canada is polite enough to conceal its thought. Mexico serenely believes Americans are yellow."

By the late nineteenth century, *yellow* and *yellow-bellied* were terms for *cowardice* in the United States, but *yellow* began as a more general expression of contempt. An 1833 citation from the *Vermont Patriot & State Gazette* refers to "true blue skin[n]ed yellow bellied federalists." The expression seems to have originated in Lincolnshire, England, where the residents of the Fens were called "yellow-bellies." Glossaries of the time suggested an allusion to local yellow-bellied eels or poor complexions.

Inhabitants of County Wexford in Ireland were also known as "yellow-bellies."

In the United States, *yellow-bellied* and *yellow* became derisive terms used during the Mexican-American War. News reports of the time referred to "yellow-bellied scoundrels" and "yellow-bellied Mexicans." Various origins have been suggested for the use of *yellow-bellied*, including the color of soldiers' uniforms, reference to snakes common to Mexico, and extension of the term *yellow dog* for a mongrel canine. However, other news reports of the 1840s referred to "yellow-skinned Mexicans," suggesting a racist origin.

Later the adjective *yellow* was used to refer to Asian immigrants and to Spanish soldiers during the Spanish-American War. The meaning of *yellow* had shifted by the twentieth century to refer to cowardice, and the term *yellow streak* emerged as well. In an 1892 citation from the New Orleans *Daily Picayune*, a writer felt the need to explain the term: "They said . . . that I had a 'yellow streak'—meaning that I was afraid."

A Man of Limited Talents from a Small Town (Warren G. Harding, 1921–1923)

Yet another Ohioan, Warren G. Harding was the owner of a newspaper in Marion and made his way to the US Senate. He had little impact as a legislator but became known as an affable conservative who enjoyed whiskey, poker,

"a cheeseparing of a man"

golf, and extramarital sex. When none of the other Republican candidates could muster a majority at their 1920 convention, the presidential-looking Harding emerged on the tenth ballot, running on the slogan "A Return to Normalcy." Harding put it this way, with his customary alliteration: "America's present need is not heroics, but healing; not nostrums, but normalcy; not revolution, but restoration; not agitation, but adjustment;

not surgery, but serenity; not the dramatic, but the dispassionate; not experiment, but equipoise; not submergence in internationality, but sustainment in triumphant nationality." Harding referred to his own speechmaking as "bloviating." William Gibbs McAdoo, Wilson's treasury secretary (and son-in-law), called Harding's speeches "an army of pompous phrases moving across the landscape in search of an idea." But Wilson's popularity was in decline, and the election became a referendum on the flagging economy and the League of Nations. Harding defeated the Democratic ticket headed by James M. Cox with a margin of almost 7 million votes.

As president, Harding deferred to Treasury Secretary Andrew Mellon, who engineered tax cuts and curtailed antitrust actions, and to Secretary of State Charles Evans Hughes, who, together with Commerce Secretary Herbert Hoover, helped American business interests compete internationally. But Harding also permitted his Ohio cronies to defraud the government. As news of the corruption and scandals began to break, Harding fell ill while traveling in the West and died of a heart attack in August 1923.

SAID OF

Harding

"a man of limited talents from a small town"—Harding's assessment of his own abilities. He later confided to a friend, "I am not fit for this office and should never have been here."

The New York Times called Harding *"a respectable Ohio politician of the second class"* when he became the Republican nominee in 1920.

Hiram Johnson, who had run as Teddy Roosevelt's vice-presidential candidate in 1912, called Harding *"a spineless sort of individual."*

"not a white man"—William Estabrook Chancellor. During Harding's career, it was sometimes suggested that Harding was part African American. A flier, addressed to the "Men and Women of America" and distributed at the 1920 Republican Convention and during the election, alleged a plot to achieve "Negro domination" of the United States. Chancellor, a professor of economics, was fired by Wooster College.

Alice Roosevelt Longworth, the daughter of the former president, made this assessment: *"Warren Harding was not a bad man. He was just a slob."*

"If ever there was a man who was a he-harlot, it was . . . Warren G. Harding."—journalist William Allen White, in a 1926 letter.

"a cheese-paring of a man"—Nicholas Butler Murray, president of Columbia University.

"a human smudge"—Clarence Darrow.

"The Vegetable"—F. Scott Fitzgerald, who wrote a 1923 play with that title about an unambitious railway clerk who becomes president. The play was viewed as satirizing Harding.

"Bungalow-minded" was how Woodrow Wilson described Harding. Wilson also said that Harding *"had a disturbingly dull mind,"* and that *"it seemed impossible to get any explanation to lodge in it."*

To Mencken, Harding had *"the intellectual grade of an aging cockroach."* And of Harding's style, Mencken said *"setting aside a college professor or two and a half a dozen dipsomaniacal newspaper reporters, . . . he writes the worst English I have ever encountered. It reminds me of a string of wet sponges; it reminds me of tattered washing on the line; it reminds me of stale bean soup, of college yells, of dogs barking idiotically through endless nights."*

At Harding's death, poet e. e. cummings wrote, *"The only man, woman or child who wrote a simple declarative sentence with seven grammatical errors is dead."*

The Bloviater

Harding is sometimes credited with inventing the word *bloviate.* He certainly popularized it, both by mention and by example, but the word had been in use from the mid-nineteenth century.

Bloviate adds the learned-sounding ending *-viate* (*abbreviate, obviate, deviate, alleviate*) to the verb *blow.* The word was a popular term in the Midwest, including Harding's home state of Ohio. The *OED* defines the word as "to talk at length, [especially] using inflated or empty rhetoric; to speechify or 'sound off.'" The word shows up in Ohio newspapers as early as the 1840s. By 1923, it occurs in no less a source than the *New York Times,* which noted: "We all like to bloviate against 'corporations.'"

In 1934, a syndicated column titled "Men Must Bloviate" held that the need for inflated rhetoric was a human one (or at least a male one): "Political platforms and love letters, campaign speeches and courtships, good government and happy marriages, are written and pursued and enjoyed in the softening haze of bloviation." The writer was Clare Boothe Brokaw, who would later become Clare Boothe Luce.

Silent Cal (Calvin Coolidge, 1923–1929)

Calvin Coolidge left his native Vermont to attend Amherst College and later to practice law in Massachusetts, rising from the city council of Northampton through the legislature to become governor in 1918. As governor, he gained attention when he used the National Guard to end a

> "nobody has ever worked harder at inactivity"

police strike, and delegates at the 1920 Republican Convention selected Coolidge for their vice presidential candidate.

So famously taciturn that he was known as "Silent Cal," Coolidge was nonetheless a savvy politician, able to use the relatively new medium of radio, the photo op, and the press conference to good advantage. His "good government" image was strengthened after he launched an investigation of the Harding scandals, and he easily won re-election in his own right in 1924 with the slogan "Keep Cool with Coolidge." Coolidge's quietude played to the stereotype of the rural New Englander but also gave the impression of a do-nothing presidency. Journalist Walter Lippmann penned a *Vanity Fair* article in which he wrote, "Nobody has ever worked harder at inactivity." Comedian Groucho Marx even joked about Coolidge's habit of taking long, daily naps. When the Coolidges attended an evening performance of *Animal Crackers*, Groucho asked, "Isn't it past your bedtime, Calvin?"

As president, Coolidge continued the policies of Treasury Secretary Mellon—reduction of taxes and minimal regulation of business—which contributed to a booming stock market. But Coolidge also failed to address the growing economic issues of farmers. He chose not to run for a second full term in 1928, retiring to Northampton, where he died five years later.

 SAID OF

Coolidge

Oswald Villard, editor of the *Nation*, called Coolidge a *"midget statesman."* Villard also quoted a Coolidge acquaintance as saying he had never met *"a man in public life so despicable, so picayune, so false to his friends as Cal."*

"that little fellow [from] Massachusetts"—Harding in 1923.

DANGEROUS CROOKED SCOUNDRELS

"the cheap veep"—Florence Harding, commenting on Coolidge's parsimony.

"probably the man of smallest caliber who has ever been made president of the United States"—the socialist *New York Call,* in one of the few negative remarks about Coolidge when he assumed the presidency after Harding's death. The *Call* added that Coolidge had "an icy hand and a heart of stone" and "the mentality of a small-town Rotarian."

A Puritan in Babylon—the title of William Allen White's 1938 biography of Coolidge, which portrayed him as "an attitude rather than an executive."

"this runty, aloof little man, who quacks when he speaks"—White's *Emporia Gazette.*

Winston Churchill considered him *a "New England backwoodsman" who would "soon sink back into the obscurity from which only accident extracted him."*

H. L. Mencken considered him *"a stubborn little fellow with a tight, unimaginative mind" and called him "a dreadful little cad."*

Alice Roosevelt Longworth said of Coolidge: *"I do wish he didn't look as if he had been weaned on a pickle."*

Hiram W. Johnson Jr., the son of the famous progressive, said Coolidge *"continually wore an expression like that of a man who just found a broken egg in his pocket."*

Wonder Boy (Herbert Hoover, 1929–1933)

Born in Iowa and raised in Oregon, Herbert Hoover pulled himself up from humble beginnings to a career as a Stanford-trained mining engineer and later the owner of silver mines in Asia. During World War I, he ran the US Food Administration, served as an adviser

"that spineless cactus at the head of the government"

to Woodrow Wilson, and later headed the European Relief and Rehabilitation Administration. A faith-based progressive, he served as the secretary of commerce for Harding and Coolidge. Harding called Hoover "the smartest gink I know." Coolidge sarcastically referred to him as "Wonder Boy" and said that Hoover "offered me unsolicited advice every day for six years, all of it bad."

When Coolidge declined to run for president in 1928, Hoover was the Republicans' choice, running on a record of prosperity that promised "a chicken in every pot and two cars in every garage." His campaign film, titled *Master of Emergencies*, touted his work as the director of relief after the 1927 flooding of the Mississippi River and portrayed him as a supremely competent administrator. Democrats remained divided over Prohibition, and Hoover easily defeated New York governor Al Smith, whom the Women's Christian Temperance League referred to as "Al-coholic Smith."

As president, Hoover began by calling Congress into a special session to address farming and tariff issues, but neither was satisfactorily resolved. Socially progressive, he was nonetheless an advocate of low taxes and a philosophical opponent of farm subsidies and of government intervention in economic matters; he had even written a book titled *American Individualism*. But his philosophy failed in the face of the scope of the worldwide Great Depression (1929–1939). By 1932, when General Douglas MacArthur turned US troops on the protesting war veterans known as the Bonus Army, the public had completely soured on Hoover. He lost badly in 1932.

Hoover felt that the press and Democrats had treated him unfairly, and in his memoirs, he included a section titled "Four Years of Personal Attacks," in which he complained of "a ceaseless torrent of ghost-written speeches supplied to Democratic Senators,

DANGEROUS CROOKED SCOUNDRELS

Congressmen, and other party leaders." He added: "A President cannot with decency and with proper regard for the dignity of his office reply to such stuff."

The association of Hoover with the Depression was a winning strategy for Democrats well after Hoover was out of office. Harry Truman, during the campaign of 1948, gave the "Hoover cart speech" at the North Carolina State Fair: "You remember the Hoover cart . . . the remains of the old tin lizzie being pulled by a mule, because you couldn't afford to buy a new car, you couldn't afford to buy gas for the old one. You remember. First you had the Hoovercrats, and then you had the Hoover carts. One always follows the other." Truman had been friendly with Hoover before the 1948 campaign; when Hoover complained about the attack, Truman replied, "Oh, that was nothing but politics."

At another stop in Boston during the campaign, Truman added, "Now, many of you recall that campaign of 1928, when Al Smith ran for president against that well-known engineer Herbert Hoover. He was one engineer who really did a job of running things backward."

 SAID OF

Hoover

Winston Churchill, who argued with Hoover in 1919 about lifting the food blockade to Germany, called Hoover "*a son-of-a-bitch.*"

"*a fascist*"—In 1929, the New York *Daily News* reported that Norman Tallentire, a prominent Communist organizer, had told a rally that "President-elect Hoover is the international leader of fascism."

"a jellyfish"—Mayor Howard Jackson of Baltimore in 1932. According to Frederick Lewis Allen in *Since Yesterday*, some prosperous conservatives "called Hoover a spineless jellyfish." And "jellyfish" was offered up as early as 1928 when the *El Paso Evening Post* ran a nickname contest for Hoover and his opponent, Al Smith.

"an irresolute and easily frightened man"—Walter Lippmann.

"that spineless cactus at the head of the government"—Governor Ross Sterling of Texas.

"inept"—Kentucky Democrat John Beckham, who referred to "two self-styled statesmen," the "inert Coolidge" and the "inept Hoover."

"a fatter, softer Coolidge" and part of the class of "shiny, shallow go-getters."—H. L. Mencken. Of Hoover's speaking style, Mencken wrote, "He is the sort of man who, if he had to recite the Twenty-Third Psalm, would make it sound like a search warrant issued under the Volstead Act."

"a recent acquisition to our population"—former Missouri senator James Reed, an Anglophobe who had long attacked Hoover as a tool of the British. The claim arose from a 1931 book called *The Strange Career of Mr. Hoover under Two Flags*, whose author later admitted to fabricating its claims.

"a big liar"—socialist Norman Thomas.

"a tyrant who happens temporarily to be president of the United States"—Wisconsin senator John Blaine.

"President Reject"—*Time* magazine, after the 1932 election.

A Kind of Amiable Boy Scout
(Franklin D. Roosevelt, 1933–1945)

Franklin D. Roosevelt grew up a child of affluent New Yorkers, attending Harvard College and studying law briefly. A distant—fifth—cousin of Teddy Roosevelt, he made his way in politics, serving in the New York State Senate before joining the Wilson

administration as assistant secretary of the
navy and running for vice president in 1920.
The next several years were consumed with
his battle against polio, which he contracted
in 1921. By 1928, he had become governor of
New York, and he soon led activist recovery

"ninety
per cent
Eleanor and
ten per cent
mush"

efforts against the Great Depression. Re-elected governor in 1930,
he was the leading contender for the 1932 Democratic nomination, winning on the fourth ballot. He easily defeated Herbert
Hoover in the general election, which also brought overwhelming
Democratic majorities to Congress.

Roosevelt promised Americans a New Deal, and his first term
was dominated by an array of bills aimed at relief efforts, renewed
industrial production, and stabilizing banks and the agricultural
economy. Two years into his administration, Roosevelt added legislation establishing a social safety net and expanding workers'
rights. Re-elected in 1936, he set out to reorganize the government
as well, including his misguided plan to pack the Supreme Court.

Hampered by the Congressional Neutrality Acts, which came
into effect as early as 1935, Roosevelt was a spectator to the
unfolding aggression by Germany and Japan. With war on the horizon, he ran for a precedent-breaking third term in 1940, with a
new vice president, Commerce Secretary Henry A. Wallace. In
early 1941, he established the Lend-Lease Program, which gave
the Allies access to American arms. After the attack on Pearl
Harbor in December 1941, the United States officially joined the
war effort, later turning the tide in the Pacific and Europe and
making plans for a postwar international order.

After the D-Day invasion in the summer of 1944, World War
II was entering its final phase. Roosevelt ran for a fourth term

in 1944 and with yet another vice president, Harry S. Truman. He defeated New York governor Thomas Dewey, who assailed Roosevelt's administration as being led by "tired old men." Roosevelt would not live to see the Germans and Japanese surrender the following year or to found the United Nations. He died in April 1945 while sitting for a portrait at his retreat in Warm Springs, Georgia.

Throughout the dozen years of his presidency, Roosevelt was insulted by both the Left and the Right, and he sometimes found early allies turning against him with angry public denunciations. Among them was the 1928 Democratic standard-bearer, Al Smith, who had joined the American Liberty League, a group of conservative Democrats and Republicans who opposed New Deal programs as socialist. Smith gave a speech equating New Dealers "with Marx and Lenin or any of the rest of that bunch." Another critic, Father Charles Coughlin, the populist anti-Semitic radio preacher, began as a Roosevelt supporter. Objecting to the low wages paid to workers in the Works Progress Administration, Coughlin called Roosevelt "a great betrayer and liar" and the "scab president."

Journalist Marquis Childs wrote a piece for *Harper's* magazine called "They Hate Roosevelt," which was later expanded as a pamphlet published by Harper & Brothers. Childs described "a consuming personal hatred of President Roosevelt" based on interviews with a handful of wealthy detractors. Roosevelt sometimes tried to win over his influential doubters personally, but at times he confronted critics, as he did in his 1936 message to Congress when he said that he "was proud to have earned the hatred of entrenched greed."

Franklin Roosevelt

"a kind of amiable Boy Scout"—journalist Walter Lippmann, who later added that the candidate was "a pleasant man who, without any important qualifications for the office, would very much like to be president."

Syndicated columnist Westbrook Pegler called Roosevelt a *"Moosejaw" and a "momma's boy."* Pegler was also the first to adapt the usage "bleeding heart" to castigate liberals.

a "chameleon on plaid"—Herbert Hoover, during the 1932 campaign. Hoover privately called Roosevelt "a gibbering idiot" and "ignorant" after meeting him during the long interregnum after the election of 1932.

a "liar and a fake"—Louisiana populist senator Huey Long in national radio broadcasts.

"a Communist [in] the chair once occupied by Washington"—Father Charles Coughlin.

"a traitor to his class"—the right-wing American Liberty League.

"the Kerensky of the American Revolutionary movement"—the Republican National Committee, attacking Roosevelt in 1936, invoking the revolutionary leader overthrown by Vladimir Lenin.

a "Wall Street tool"—Earl Browder, leader of the US Communist Party.

"crazy, conceited megalomaniac"—Michigan congressman Clare Hoffman.

"the prize honeyfuggler of his time"—the *Syracuse Herald* in 1934, revisiting Taft's characterization of Teddy Roosevelt.

Alice Roosevelt Longworth was said to have characterized Franklin Roosevelt as *"ninety per cent Eleanor and ten per cent mush."* She denied that she had used the term *mush*, and, in her obituary, the *New York Times* gave the quote as "one-third sap and two-thirds Eleanor."

To H. L. Mencken, Roosevelt was *"a Quack,"* and the New Deal was a *"political racket"* and a *"series of stupendous bogus miracles."* Mencken said that if the president, whom he referred to as "Roosevelt the Minor," "became convinced tomorrow that coming out for cannibalism would get him the votes he so sorely needs, he would begin fattening a missionary in the White House."

"an utter incompetent"—Supreme Court justice John C. McReynolds. McReynolds's colleague, Justice Oliver Wendell Holmes, is often cited as saying that Roosevelt had "a second-class intellect, but a first-class temperament," though he may have actually been referring to Teddy Roosevelt.

Bund leader Fritz Kuhn held a Nazi rally in Madison Square Garden in early 1939 in which he referred to FDR as *"Frank D. Rosenfeld"* and to the New Deal as the *"Jew Deal."*

"a lawless dictator"—Republican congressman George Tinkham of Massachusetts in 1940, after Roosevelt signed the destroyers-for-bases deal without submitting it to Congress.

a *"dictator"*—*Little House on the Prairie* writer Laura Ingalls Wilder, in a letter to her daughter, Rose Wilder Lane, who later became a founder of the libertarian movement.

"that crippled son-of-a-bitch that killed my son Joe"—Ambassador Joseph Kennedy. Harry Truman reported that he threatened to throw Kennedy out a window for saying that.

The attacks kept coming even after FDR's death. Ruth Alexander, a columnist for Hearst's New York Mirror, gave a speech in 1959 in which she referred to FDR as a *"rainy-day plutocrat"* and to Eleanor Roosevelt as *"his buck-toothed bride."*

ETYMOLOGICAL EXPLORATIONS

Socialists All

The earliest uses of the word *socialist*, from the late eighteenth century and now obsolete, meant a person living in a civilized society. By the middle of the nineteenth century, *socialist* had gained a political meaning, referring broadly to the social control of income and property. Socialism today comes in a variety of forms, from social democratic approaches based on government regulation and strong tax-supported social programs, to authoritarian approaches involving centralized state control and government ownership of industries.

Progressives such as Theodore Roosevelt and Woodrow Wilson were sometimes dubbed socialists, as was the populist William Jennings Bryan, who ran as a Democrat in 1896, 1900, and 1904. The actual Socialists didn't see it that way. At the beginning of the twentieth century, various socialist and reform factions unified for a time behind Eugene V. Debs, who ran in 1900, 1904, 1908, 1912, and 1920. In two of those elections, Debs garnered over nine hundred thousand votes, with support from union members, reformers, farmers, and immigrants. It was the best showing ever for a Socialist Party candidate.

For many years, socialism and communism were twin foils for American politicians attempting to delay or turn back the clock of social reform. In 1936, the *Chicago Tribune* published a two-part story titled "Is Roosevelt a Socialist?" (The writer's answer was "Yes.") Truman was described as the head of a "socialist-labor regime," and Westbrook Pegler would even refer to "Eisenhower's socialist-Republican Party." When Lyndon Johnson ran as John F. Kennedy's vice president, Southern critics complained that he had "sold out to Yankee socialists." Conservative California Republicans even took issue with Richard Nixon's "socialist budget" when he was president.

Today, with the Union of Soviet Socialist Republics in the rearview mirror, socialism has new momentum among millennials. Media reports indicate that membership in the Democratic Socialists of America grew from six thousand in 2016 to nearly forty thousand in 2018. But the Gallup organization also notes that Democratic-leaning and Republican-leaning voters still have very different opinions about the meaning of *socialism*, with Republican-leaners about twice as likely to see socialism as involving government control or "modified communism."

Whether *socialist* continues to be an effective line of attack in presidential elections remains to be seen. Based on history, there is little doubt that it will continue to be used.

"An oratorical mortician"

SIX

A World Power, 1945–1980

A s World War II ended, the United States emerged as the indispensable global police officer—the Cold War coun- terpart to the Soviet Union and China. At the same time, the country grew up domestically, its postwar economy supporting the expansion of housing, education, and the mass media and its postwar awakening fostering advances in civil rights and social reform. The nation struggled through the McCarthyism of the 1950s, and the New Deal was extended by the Great Society programs of the 1960s. The country engaged in undeclared wars in Korea in the early 1950s and in Vietnam during the 1960s and early 1970s, the latter sparking antiwar protests and a countercul- ture movement. A president would resign in the face of almost certain impeachment. The era began when Franklin Roosevelt's third vice president took the oath of office on April 12, 1945.

A Vulgar Little Babbitt (Harry S. Truman, 1945–1953)

Harry Truman served just eighty-two days as vice president, having been selected for the job in large part because he was a Southerner. Truman had been a farmer, a small businessman, a National Guard soldier in World War I, and a haberdasher before getting involved in politics. In the 1920s he served as a county judge and was elected in 1934 as a US senator with the backing of the political boss of Kansas City, Missouri, Thomas Pendergast. Known in the Senate for chairing an investigation of defense spending during World War II, Truman replaced Vice President Henry A. Wallace, who had lost the support of Democratic leaders.

> "invariably awkward, uninspired, and above all mediocre"

Truman was a talented administrator but suffered by comparison with the larger-than-life Roosevelt. The Republican Party mocked him in 1946 with the slogan "To Err is Truman" and the question "Had Enough?" Republicans took control of Congress that year, and Truman seemed headed for certain defeat in 1948. However, his folksy style and outreach to key constituencies enabled him to hold the New Deal coalition together despite independent candidacies from Wallace (running on the Progressive Party ticket) and Strom Thurmond (running as a States Rights' Party candidate). Truman ran against a "Do-Nothing Congress" and eked out a 49.5 percent victory in the popular vote.

Truman could bristle at personal attacks—he famously threatened to punch a reviewer who said his daughter could not sing well—and in later memoirs and campaigns made candid assessments of Eisenhower, Nixon, and Kennedy. As the nation succumbed to the fear of communists in government, and Senator Joseph McCarthy launched his famous hunt for subversives in 1950, Truman was mocking but publicly measured. At a 1950 news conference, Truman said, "I think the greatest asset that the Kremlin has is Senator McCarthy." In a letter sent the following day to Secretary of State Dean Acheson, Truman wrote, "Privately, I refer to McCarthy as a pathological liar, and [Senator

Kenneth] Wherry as the block-headed undertaker from Nebraska. Of course, we can't do that publicly, but there's no doubt that's exactly what they are."

Truman received the blame for the postwar challenges of a peacetime economy: expectations of full employment and higher wages. Instead, prices increased and a series of strikes affected key industries. Truman's efforts to desegregate the armed forces and to prohibit discrimination in the civil service provoked harsh reaction from white Southerners, and his attempt to expand the New Deal was stymied.

Truman choose not to run again in 1952.

 SAID OF

Truman

"*Pendergast's bell hop*"—Kansas City boss Thomas J. Pendergast, who was eventually jailed for tax evasion related to bribes.

"*a vulgar little Babbitt*"—publisher Henry Luce, referring to the 1930 Sinclair Lewis novel about the middle class.

A *Time* magazine cover story in 1948 referred to Truman as a "*political accident*," adding that his performance in office was "*invariably awkward, uninspired, and above all mediocre.*"

"*a son-of-a-bitch*"—Senator Joseph McCarthy, in 1951.

"*a monster*" and "*the butcher of Asia*"—Writer Zora Neale Hurston called Truman this in a letter to a friend, referring to the dropping of atomic bombs on Japan.

"*a nincompoop*"—The *Chicago Daily Tribune* referred to Truman this way in a front-page editorial in 1948, after he had criticized it as one of the two worst papers in the country. The *Tribune* also published the (incorrect) postelection headline "Dewey Defeats Truman" on November 3.

"a gutter fighter"—General Douglas MacArthur, in a 1954 interview, published after MacArthur's death.

"malicious"—columnist Westbrook Pegler, who said, "I recognize the type now. You see them out West. Thin-lipped, a hater, a bad man in a fight. Malicious and unforgiving."

"a phony like Roosevelt"—Pegler. Truman considered Pegler a "rat" and a "guttersnipe."

"a traitor"—Richard Nixon, campaigning in 1952 when McCarthyism was at its height. He called Truman, Dean Acheson, and Adlai Stevenson "traitors to the high principles in which many of the nation's Democrats believe." Nixon was referring to charges that the State Department had been infiltrated by Communists, and he went on to say that "real Democrats are outraged by the Truman-Acheson-Stevenson gang's toleration and defense of Communism in high places." In his later interviews with Merle Miller, Truman said of Nixon, "I don't think the son-of-a-bitch knows the difference between telling the truth and lying."

A Dime-Store New Dealer
(Dwight Eisenhower, 1953–1961)

Dwight Eisenhower graduated from the US Military Academy at West Point and served under Generals Douglas MacArthur and George C. Marshall. By 1944 he was supreme commander of Operation Overlord, which

> "a nice old gentleman in a golf cart"

launched the D-Day invasion. After World War II, Eisenhower served as army chief of staff, as president of Columbia University, and then as the first supreme commander of North Atlantic Treaty Organization (NATO) forces in Europe. In 1952 he declared himself a Republican; he won the presidency that year and re-election in 1956, defeating Adlai Stevenson both times.

As president, Eisenhower declined to roll back the New Deal and even expanded Social Security. He signed the first civil rights legislation, providing new federal voting rights, and he enforced the Supreme Court's desegregation decision in *Brown v. Board of Education* (1954). His quiet approach was successful politically, keeping the administration from being the focus of attention on a wide variety of issues. But Eisenhower's moderation angered both conservatives, who hoped he would reverse the New Deal, and progressives, who hoped for stronger leadership on civil rights.

Eisenhower also avoided confronting Joseph McCarthy directly, instead letting him self-destruct. In his diary, Eisenhower wrote, "Nothing will be so effective in combating his particular kind of trouble-making as to ignore him. This he cannot stand."

Internationally, Eisenhower used the Central Intelligence Agency (CIA) covertly to challenge Soviet initiatives—and in some cases to overthrow governments—while also courting non-aligned nations and pursuing summit opportunities. In Southeast Asia, he continued the aid program to the French in Indochina, and after the French withdrawal, his administration worked to establish what would later become South Vietnam.

 SAID OF

Eisenhower

In 1947 General Douglas MacArthur referred to Eisenhower as *"the best clerk I ever had."* Eisenhower in turn noted that he had "studied theatrics under MacArthur."

"Dopey Dwight"—William Loeb, publisher of the Manchester (New Hampshire) *Union Leader*. His paper's sneering right-wing editorials attacked politicians from Truman to George H. W. Bush, and as the only statewide newspaper in the first-in-the-nation primary state, Loeb's

publication had an outsized impact on political discourse. Loeb also called Eisenhower "a stinking hypocrite," a "playboy president," and a "fathead."

a *"good-looking mortician"*—David Ingalls, the campaign manager for Robert Taft, Eisenhower's 1952 opponent for the nomination. Ingalls also called Eisenhower "a pig in a poke" and urged Republicans not to choose on the basis of "hero worship," "glamour," or "sex appeal."

a *"stooge"*—Harry Truman, campaigning for Stevenson in 1952. He called Eisenhower "a front man for an unholy crew" of lobbyists and added that Stevenson was not a "stooge for Wall Street." Truman also privately called Eisenhower a "coward" for failing to confront Joseph McCarthy and referred to him as "that dumb son-of-a-bitch Eisenhower."

a *"puppet"*—Republican senator Wayne Morse of Oregon. Endorsing Stevenson in 1952, Morse said Eisenhower was "dangling and dancing . . . at the end of political puppet strings being jerked by some of the most evil and reactionary forces in American politics."

"the yellow son-of-a-bitch!"—*Washington Post* columnist Joseph Alsop to a colleague, after listening to Eisenhower's 1954 news conference in which he failed to condemn Joseph McCarthy by name.

a *"part-time president" who conducted "an indifferent administration"*—Adlai Stevenson in 1956.

"a dime-store New Dealer"—Arizona Republican Barry Goldwater, when Eisenhower proposed a program of highway construction during his administration.

a *"Communist agent"*—Robert Welch, founder of the far-right John Birch Society. Welch called Eisenhower "a dedicated, conscious agent of the communist conspiracy" and added, "The chances are very strong that Milton Eisenhower [Ike's brother and the president of Johns Hopkins University] is actually Dwight Eisenhower's boss and superior in the Communist Party."

"that old asshole"—John F. Kennedy, privately. Eisenhower, for his part, considered Kennedy merely a "pretty boy" and "a young whippersnapper," and referred to him as "Little Boy Blue."

"devious"—In his 1962 book *Six Crises,* Richard Nixon wrote that Eisenhower was "far more complex and devious than most Americans realize." Nixon said he meant it as a compliment.

"the worst president of the United States with the possible exception of James Buchanan"—Joseph Alsop. Alsop also called Eisenhower "a nice old gentleman in a golf cart" and compared him to "a dead whale on a beach." Eisenhower called Alsop "the lowest form of animal life on the earth."

ETYMOLOGICAL EXPLORATIONS

From Jackass to Asshole

When newspapers of his day referred to John Tyler as "The Executive Ass," they were comparing him to an animal. *Ass,* the word for the beast of burden, is a Celtic borrowing into Old English. In Middle and Early Modern English, *ass* was commonly used to refer to a fool as well, such as in the *Merry Wives of Windsor* when Slender remarks to Falstaff that "though I cannot remember what I did when you made me drunke, yet I am not altogether an asse." John Tyler was also called a "jackass." That compound emerged in the eighteenth century as both a synonym for the animal and as an insult.

Ass in the sense of buttocks is inherited from Germanic and famously attested in Chaucer's "Miller's Tale," whose narrator relates of Absolon and Alison that "with his mouth he kist her nakid Ers." Later the word was spelled *arse,* and in r-less British dialects it was pronounced more or less like *ass.* That pronunciation and the r-less spelling became the norm in America, making the two meanings of *ass* homonyms.

The compound *asshole* for anus is attested in the nineteenth century and soon became a geographic metaphor for an area considered remote or extremely unpleasant. By the post-World War II era, an *asshole* could also be a person, who was, as the *OED* explains, "stupid, irritating, or contemptible." This was the sense that John F. Kennedy had in mind when he privately called Dwight Eisenhower "that old asshole." And as Geoffrey

Nunberg noted in his study *Assholism: The Ascent of the A-Word*, the epithet *asshole* made its serious literary debut in Norman Mailer's 1948 novel *The Naked and the Dead*, describing a certain lieutenant who was "a perfect asshole" in his naïve self-importance.

A Little Scrawny Fellow with Rickets
(John F. Kennedy, 1961–1963)

The son of a wealthy ambassador and grandson of a Boston mayor, John F. Kennedy grew up in privilege. He graduated from Harvard College in 1940, turning his senior thesis into a bestselling book called *Why England Slept*. After serving in combat as commander of a PT boat in World War II, Kennedy won election to the House of Representatives in 1946 and to the Senate in 1952. Though Kennedy's health had been poor since his youth, he managed to project an image of vigor and made a run for the vice presidency in 1956, which along with his membership on the Senate Foreign Relations Committee, positioned him for the 1960 election. That year, Kennedy defeated Minnesota's Hubert Humphrey in a series of primaries and won the nomination on the first ballot, choosing another rival, Senate majority leader Lyndon Johnson, as his running mate. He won a razor-thin victory over Nixon in the general election.

> "the enviably attractive nephew who winsomely disappears before the table-clearing and dishwashing begin"

Kennedy had good relations with the press, which ignored his many sexual indiscretions, and he tended to respond to criticism and attacks with humor. When Richard Nixon called him "another Truman," Kennedy responded that he was flattered and said,

"I consider Mr. Nixon another Dewey," referring to Truman's 1948 Republican opponent.

Kennedy's New Frontier—a combination of education, health, and urban and rural development programs—met with congressional skepticism, and his cautious response to civil rights issues displeased both Southern Democrats and African American leaders. Internationally, Kennedy faced challenges in Berlin, Cuba, and Southeast Asia, but achieved a nuclear test ban agreement.

On November 22, 1963, Kennedy was assassinated, being struck by two bullets while riding in a motorcade in Dallas, Texas. His New Frontier agenda would become the Great Society of his successor, Lyndon Johnson.

 SAID OF

Kennedy

"a goddamn Mick"—John "Black Jack" Bouvier, Kennedy's future father-in-law, after their first meeting, using a derisive term for an Irishman (a shortening of the name Michael).

a "little scrawny fellow with rickets"—Lyndon Johnson, in an interview with a reporter for the *Chicago Daily News* in 1960, spreading rumors about Kennedy's health. At the time, the two were rivals for the Democratic nomination.

"Papa's pet"—Hubert Humphrey in 1960, when he was competing for the Democratic nomination. Humphrey also complained that Kennedy was acting "like a spoiled juvenile."

"a spoiled young man"—Harry Truman.

"the enviably attractive nephew who sings an Irish ballad for the company, and then winsomely disappears before the table-clearing and dishwashing begin."—Harry McPherson, a Johnson speechwriter, attributing the sentiment to Johnson.

"the young genius"—Dwight Eisenhower, being ironic. He also called Kennedy a "wizard of shell games."

"not a man's man"—Lyndon Johnson.

"a barefaced liar"—Richard Nixon.

"Calamity Jack" and *"the No. 1 liar in the United States"*—publisher William Loeb.

a *"military dictator"*—Alabama governor George Wallace, whom Kennedy confronted over integration.

"a compromiser with evil"—Roy Wilkins, head of the National Association for the Advancement of Colored People, criticizing Kennedy's cautious approach to civil rights. Wilkins described Kennedy's proposals as "a cactus bouquet."

a *"traitor"*—General Charles P. Cabel, a deputy director of the CIA who was fired by Kennedy after the 1961 Bay of Pigs invasion failed.

When Kennedy visited Dallas in 1963, protesters distributed about five thousand copies of what became known as the *"treason handbill."* Under photos of Kennedy, the flier's text said Kennedy was *"wanted for treasonous activities against the United States of America."*

"more wicked than Hitler"—philosopher Bertrand Russell, when Kennedy resumed nuclear testing in 1962.

The B Is for . . . (Lyndon B. Johnson, 1963–1969)

Lyndon Baines Johnson grew up in rural Texas, one of five siblings in a financially strapped family. After trying his hand at teaching, he made his way to politics. Johnson was elected to the House in 1937 and to the Senate in 1948, rising to its leadership in the 1950s.

"a real centaur— part man, part horse's ass"

Supporters in the South felt betrayed when Johnson joined Kennedy's ticket in 1960. Herman Brown, a Texas construction entrepreneur who was LBJ's chief financial supporter, called him "a goddam traitor." Southern newspapers, angered by Johnson's advocacy of civil rights, referred to him as "a southern Benedict Arnold," "a Texas Yankee," and a "political polygamist." In Texas, crowds shouted "Judas candidate" at him, and the state's sole Republican congressman showed up at one rally holding a sign that read "LBJ sold out to Yankee Socialists."

Sworn in after Kennedy's assassination, Johnson launched the set of initiatives called the Great Society and won election in his own right in 1964, defeating Senator Barry Goldwater.

His domestic legislative accomplishments included Medicare, Medicaid, Head Start, and the War on Poverty. Johnson also won the passage of a series of civil rights bills, though racial tensions grew in several major cities. Internationally, Johnson found himself mired in the Vietnam War, which escalated to a commitment of five hundred thousand troops and by the end saw over fifty-eight thousand casualties.

Johnson largely maintained a stoic, even hangdog, public mask as criticism mounted, but privately seethed. *Time* magazine reported that in one confrontation in 1967, Senator Robert Kennedy had called the president a "son-of-a-bitch" in a meeting. Kennedy denied this but told reporter Jack Newfield that the meeting "wasn't very pleasant" and that Johnson was "mean," "abusive," and "seemed very unstable."

As the war dragged on and became ever more divisive at home, Johnson faced challenges within his own party and declined to seek a second full term.

Lyndon Johnson

"Lyndon Benedict Johnson"—a speaker at the Dallas Democratic Party meeting attended by Kennedy and Johnson. The speaker also referred to Kennedy as "Mister Boston Beans," invoking Boston's traditional dish of beans slow-cooked in molasses.

"a faker"—Barry Goldwater. Johnson was, according to Goldwater, "the phoniest individual who ever came along" and "a scheming wire puller," whose residence should be renamed "the Whitewash House." He also called Johnson an "interim president" conducting a "lie-filled campaign." Johnson referred to Goldwater as "a raving, ranting demagogue."

a *"mad wild dog"*—H. Rap Brown, the head of the Student Non-violent Coordinating Committee, who saw Johnson as emblematic of an oppressive ruling class. Brown also referred to him "a white honky character" and an "outlaw from Texas."

Virginia congressman Howard Smith, who had tried to stall the Voting Rights Act of 1965, called Johnson a *"rattlesnake"* who harbored a *"great hatred for the South"* and was trying to punish his native region.

Dean Acheson, who had been Truman's secretary of state, called Johnson *"a real centaur—part man, part horse's ass."*

a *"bully with an Air Force"*—writer Norman Mailer. As Vietnam casualties mounted and the war seemed unresolvable, Mailer saw Johnson as "close to insanity."

"der Fuehrer"—Marie Harriman, wife of W. Averell Harriman, a US ambassador-at-large and later Johnson's representative to the Paris Peace talks.

"Dr. Cornpone"—William F. Buckley, among others (including some former Kennedy aides), referring to Johnson's accent and Texas style.

"the big fool"—Folk singer Pete Seeger, performing on the *Smothers Brothers Comedy Hour* in 1967. His song "Waist Deep in the Big Muddy" alluded to Johnson as "the big fool" who insisted on pushing on. Johnson had previously complained about the Smothers Brothers, reportedly

calling the head of CBS in the middle of the night and telling him to "Get those bastards off my back." When Seeger was scheduled to perform "Waist Deep in the Big Muddy" on the show in September 1967, CBS censored the performance.

"a liar"—Historian Robert Caro reports that Johnson's college classmates referred to him as "Bullshit Johnson" because, as one classmate put it, he was "the biggest liar on campus." During Johnson's administration, the expression "credibility gap" (which first appeared in print in 1963) came to be widely used to indicate doubts about the truthfulness of his administration.

"that bastard Johnson"—Vice President Hubert Humphrey, when Johnson refused to see him in 1968.

Tricky Dick (Richard Nixon, 1969–1974)

Richard Nixon served in the navy during World War II and made his way to the House of Representatives in 1946 and to the Senate in 1950. His campaigns earned him the nickname Tricky Dick, and Nixon was selected as Eisenhower's running mate in 1952, remaining on the ticket despite the last-minute exposé of a slush fund. Nixon suffered a narrow defeat for the presidency in 1960 and then decisively lost a bid for California's governorship in 1962. He re-emerged as the "new Nixon" in 1968, capturing the White House over Hubert Humphrey and third-party candidate George Wallace.

"a swine of a man and a jabbering dupe of a president"

Nixon eased Cold War tensions, notably with his opening to China and policy of détente with the Soviet Union, but found himself unable to end the war in Vietnam. He viewed antiwar protests and the counterculture as a threat and even briefly approved a plan to use intelligence services to disrupt protest organizations. His administration also had a twenty-item enemies list that named journalists, politicians, labor leaders, and others, including actor Paul Newman. The enemies list grew longer, and Nixon speechwriter William Safire referred to Nixon as "the first political paranoid with a majority!"

Nixon's downfall came about after five men connected to his Special Investigations Unit (nicknamed the "Plumbers") were arrested in June 1972 for breaking into the Democratic Party headquarters at the Watergate Hotel. The secret unit had been operating since 1971, and the administration had been covering up its existence and activities, such as break-ins, bugging, and other political dirty tricks. The efforts of the Plumbers and details of the cover-up were captured on White House tape recordings between Nixon and his aides and led to a constitutional crisis. After Nixon fired special prosecutor Archibald Cox, his successor, Leon Jaworski, won the release of the tapes in an 8-0 Supreme Court decision. The "smoking gun tape" captured a conversation just days after the Watergate break-in; in it Nixon agreed that administration officials should try to stop the Federal Bureau of Investigation (FBI) investigation. With the revelations on the tapes, Nixon's congressional support eroded, and he resigned on August 9, 1974.

 SAID OF

Nixon

a "demagogue"—Helen Gahagan Douglas, Nixon's 1950 Senate opponent. She said he relied on "fear and . . . nice, unadulterated fascism." Her campaign literature called Nixon a "Peewee trying to frighten people" and referred to "the backwash of Republican young men in dark shirts," an allusion to Hitler's brown shirts.

"a well-oiled drawbridge between McCarthyite barbarism and Eisenhower respectability"—writer Irving Howe, founder of the magazine *Dissent*, referring to Nixon's role as a hatchet-man of the anti-Communist right.

"the white-collar McCarthy"—Adlai Stevenson.

"a no-good lying bastard"—former president Harry Truman in 1960, adding that anyone who voted for Nixon "ought to go to hell."

"a filthy lying son-of-a-bitch and a very dangerous man"—John F. Kennedy in 1960.

a *"two-fisted four-square liar"*—Barry Goldwater, writing about Nixon's concessions to liberal Republicans in the 1960 platform.

"a traitor" to conservatism—Paul Weyrich, conservative activist and co-founder of the Heritage Foundation.

"He's a cheap bastard. That's all there is to it."—Kennedy to journalist Ben Bradlee.

"a swine of a man and a jabbering dupe of a president"—Gonzo journalist Hunter S. Thompson.

"the Mad Monk"—Nixon aide John Ehrlichman, referring to Nixon's penchant for brooding.

"meatball mind"—Secretary of State Henry Kissinger, who also privately referred to Nixon as "our drunken friend" and "that madman."

"Nixon's a shit"—Gerald Ford's national security adviser Brent Scowcroft, on learning that Nixon would visit China before the 1976 election. The announcement of Nixon's trip, just days before the New Hampshire primary, was seen as a slap in the face to Ford, who had adopted a go-slow policy on normalizing relations.

A Ford, Not a Lincoln (Gerald Ford, 1974–1977)

When Gerald Ford became president on August 9, 1974, he told the nation that its constitutional ordeal was over, but he also lowered expectations, saying he was "a Ford, not a Lincoln." A football star in his youth, Ford served in World War II, earned a law degree from Yale, and practiced law in his native Michigan before winning election to the House of Representatives in 1948. He remained there, rising to minority leader, until he was selected by Nixon to replace Vice President Spiro Agnew.

"a nice guy who played too much football with his helmet off"

During Ford's two-plus years as president, the economy continued to unravel due to inflation, unemployment, and rising oil prices, and Ford faced solid Democratic majorities in Congress. And thanks in part to his own physical stumbles—such as falling down the steps of *Air Force One*—and their portrayal on a new television show called *Saturday Night Live*, Ford was caricatured as bumbling and ineffectual.

Stung by the caricatures, Ford noted that "though it was essential to grin and bear it, it could and did hurt." In a 1987 book on humor in politics, he wrote, "The portrayal of me as an oafish ex-jock made for good copy. It was also funny. Maybe not to me, but as much as I might have disliked it, some people were laughing."

A month into his presidency, Ford issued an unconditional pardon for Nixon, which hurt his re-election chances. In 1976 he faced a primary challenge from former California governor Ronald Reagan, and he lost the general election to a little-known Georgia politician named Jimmy Carter.

SAID OF

Ford

"a nice guy who played too much football with his helmet off"—Lyndon Johnson, alluding to Ford's intellect. Johnson also said that Ford was "so dumb, he can't fart and chew gum at the same time."

William Loeb dubbed Gerald Ford *"Jerry the jerk"* and compared him to Brutus betraying Caesar. The alliterative Loeb also referred to Ford's wife as "Babbling Betty."

a "dumb bastard"—industrialist and Reagan confidant Justin Dart, speaking to the *Los Angeles Times*. Dart later apologized to Ford.

"a fine-looking man in a Lake Wobegon sort of way"—Harvard sociologist Orlando Patterson, in a *New York Times* op-ed essay.

"Eisenhower without medals"— Ford aide Jerry terHorst, apparently meant as a compliment.

"Old Bungle Foot"—*New York Post* columnist Nicholas von Hoffman, who also referred to Ford as "Mr. Ten Thumbs," "America's Pet Rock," and "catastrophically close to making himself into a national clown."

"slow, unimaginative and not very articulate"—journalist Richard Reeves in his book *A Ford, Not a Lincoln*, referring to Ford's rise as "a triumph of lowest-common-denominator politics, the survival of the man without enemies, the least objectionable alternative."

a "cynical, clumsy and arrogant political bully"—Geraldo Rivera at a political rally in 1975, after Ford rejected the idea of federal assistance to save New York City from bankruptcy.

"worse than Harding and Hoover put together"—Democrat Tip O'Neill, then House majority leader.

Jerktown

When William Loeb called Gerald Ford "Jerry the Jerk," he was deploying some early-twentieth-century slang. The early linguistic history of the term *jerk* suggests gullibility. A. J. Pollock's *Underworld Speaks* (1935) includes a description of *jerk* as "a boob; chump; a sucker," but a 1938 *New Republic* piece by Heywood Hale Broun explains, "A stuffed shirt is a pretentious bore. A jerk not only bores you but pats you on the shoulder as he does so."

The word *jerk* quickly became an indication of personality as well as intelligence, and its use to refer to someone annoying or even contemptible was well established by the 1950s. *Jerk* became a favorite word of Ernest Hemingway, who used it nearly a dozen times in dialogue in *Across the River and into the Trees*.

Where does the word *jerk* come from? A possible source is the nineteenth-century expression "a jerkwater train," which referred to the early railroad custom of pulling (or jerking) water from streams to fill the boiler. Later that practice was relegated to smaller branch trains, which became known as "jerkwater trains." The word was extended to indicate both remote location and insignificance: *jerk* as slang for a chump or sucker may have suggested someone from a jerkwater town or, as later slang had it, *Jerktown*.

Other possible influences or sources include the expression "the jerks," used to refer to "nervous, ecstatic, or delirious twitching." *Los Angeles Times* columnist Timothy Turner included a fictitious character named "Jerry the Jerk" in columns published in 1943.

"Jerking" was also nineteenth-century slang for masturbation. Jonathan Lighter's *Random House Historical Dictionary of American Slang* cites a claim that *jerk* originated as "a derogatory name first applied by burlesque performers to members of their audience."

Mr. Peanut (Jimmy Carter, 1977–1981)

Jimmy Carter graduated from the US Naval Academy in 1946 as an engineer, and he was part of the team that developed the first nuclear-powered submarines. Carter returned to Georgia in the 1950s to take over the family peanut farm and became involved in local politics. By the early 1960s he was a Georgia state senator, and he ran in the Democratic primary for governor in 1966, losing to segregationist Lester Maddox. Tacking to the right to court conservative white voters, Carter won the governorship in 1970. He announced his candidacy for the presidency at the end of 1974. Initially dismissed as "a pig in a poke," he eventually outperformed better-known Democrats in the primaries and defeated Gerald Ford in the general election.

> "an out-and-out leftist coated over and disguised with peanut oil"

Carter's presidency saw successes in energy policy in the wake of rising oil prices, though his efforts were sometimes undermined by his own party in Congress. Public perception of Carter as moralizing and micromanaging made him an easy target; he was called "Jimmy Hoover" at one point, linking him with the thirty-first president in more than just a common engineering background.

Foreign affairs issues such as the Iran hostage crisis, which began in November 1979; the Soviet invasion of Afghanistan in December 1979; and even the debate over control of the Panama Canal in 1977 and 1978 created an impression of weakness. Carter eventually faced a challenge from within his own party by Senator Edward Kennedy, and he went on to lose the 1980 general election.

Carter

"a Dr. Jekyll and Mr. Hyde"—Georgia governor Lester Maddox.

a *"smiling hypocrite"*—Carl Sanders, Carter's 1970 Democratic primary opponent for the governorship. Sanders also called Carter "a liar," "a phony," "a user of political snake oil," and "an unprincipled grinning chameleon."

"a dangerous man"—George McGovern, the 1972 Democratic standard-bearer, as Carter was closing in on the nomination in 1976.

a *"Southern-fried McGovern"*—Republican vice presidential candidate Bob Dole, in 1976.

"a Reagan clone"—Senator Edward Kennedy, running against Carter in 1980. Kennedy also called Carter "the worst failure of presidential leadership in fifty years."

an *"oratorical mortician who inters his words and ideas beneath piles of syntactical mush"*—former senator Eugene McCarthy.

a *"Missionary lectern-pounding Amen ten-finger C-major-chord Sister-Martha-at-the-Yamaha-keyboard loblolly piney-woods Baptist."*—writer Tom Wolfe. *Loblolly* is a dialect term for both a bumpkin and a mudhole.

"a complete birdbrain"—Republican congressman John Leboutillier in 1981.

"a goddamn liar"—Texas governor William Clements in 1980.

"the biggest flip-flopper I know of"—Gerald Ford, during the 1976 campaign.

"a little schmuck"—Ronald Reagan, during the 1980 campaign.

an *"out-and-out leftist coated over and disguised with peanut oil"*—William Loeb, who also called Carter "stupid" and "an incompetent little man."

a *"waste of skin"*—Conservative media personality Glenn Beck on the 2006 radio premiere of *The Glenn Beck Program*.

"a disaster"—Gerald Ford in his posthumously published interviews.

"Poor dear, there's nothing between his ears"

SEVEN

Culture Wars, 1980–2018

As the twentieth century entered its final two decades, the World Wide Web and the Internet were on the horizon, and the first two-pound mobile telephone was a few years away from being marketed. By 2016, those early phones had evolved into the now-ubiquitous smartphones, and the Internet was used by nearly 90 percent of American adults, with two-thirds using some form of social media. The way people received information had changed.

Ted Turner's twenty-four-hour Cable News Network (CNN) was founded in 1980, challenging the dominance of the network television opinion makers. The repeal of the Federal Communications Commission's Fairness Doctrine in 1987 further fueled the growth of partisan talk radio and partisan cable news. MSNBC, Fox News, and the *Daily Show* all began in 1996.

The funding of political messages evolved as well. Changes in campaign financing and the growth of political action committees created opportunities for more advertising and more negativity. Political messaging became increasingly sophisticated, moving beyond simply mobilizing a base to push polling, big data demographics, and targeted fake news. It was a return to the partisan press of the late 1700s.

The Grinning Gallant (Ronald Reagan, 1981–1989)

A crowded Republican field was taking aim at Jimmy Carter in 1980. By March of that year, only three contenders remained: Ronald Reagan, George H. W. Bush, and Illinois congressman John Anderson, who went on to run as an independent in the general election.

"a petrified pig, unfit to govern"

Reagan seemed an unlikely candidate. Born in 1911, he was already in his late sixties and had been an actor for much of his career, serving at one point as president of the Screen Actors Guild. Originally a liberal Democrat, Reagan became a Republican only in the 1960s but soon was campaigning for right-wing candidates in California and was co-chairman of California Citizens for Goldwater.

In 1966 Reagan won his first-ever political campaign, for governor of California, running against high taxes and a "morality gap," taking special aim at student activism at the University of California at Berkeley and at public assistance programs. In an October 1966 cover story called "Ronald for Real," *Time* magazine described him this way:

> In the course of 50 movies, Ronald Wilson Reagan almost invariably played the grinning gallant, the fall guy who winds up heartbroken, dead broke or plain dead. In *King's Row*, he lost his legs; in *Santa Fe Trail* and *Dark Victory*, bigger stars got the girl. In *Hellcats of the Navy*, he wound up taking a submarine on a suicidal mission; as George Gipp in *Knute Rockne—All American*, he expired exhorting the team to greater glory. So indelibly was Reagan type-cast as the Great Loser that when Movie Magnate Jack Warner, his

longtime employer, was first apprised of the actor's ambition to run for Governor of California, he protested: "No, Jimmy Stewart for Governor. Ronald Reagan for Best Friend."

Yet in the first of his two terms as governor, Reagan was already being touted as a future presidential hopeful. In 1968 he ran as part of a "stop Nixon" movement, and in 1976 he challenged incumbent Gerald Ford. Four years later, Reagan finally sealed the nomination, and he sailed to victory over Jimmy Carter. Reagan had crafted a folksy, homespun image, but he also relied on opposition to international communism, proposals for tax cuts and deregulation, and a set of culture war themes. Surviving an assassination attempt just two months into his presidency, Reagan enjoyed a somewhat extended honeymoon period, and his likeability in the face of disapproval led Colorado Democrat Patricia Schroeder to refer to him as "the Teflon-coated President." Reagan never responded to the characterization, but the name "Teflon president" stuck. He was re-elected in 1984, carrying every state except Minnesota. Reagan's second term was occupied with revelations of covert arms sales to Iran, along with a tax payer-funded bailout of the savings-and-loan industry. Nevertheless, leaving office in 1989, Reagan held an approval rating of 68 percent.

SAID OF

Reagan

an "extremist," "an enemy of the people" with "a pathological fear of government"—Governor Edmund G. ("Pat") Brown, running against Reagan in 1966.

"a petrified pig, unfit to govern"—Berkeley sociologist Harry Edwards, after then-governor Reagan called for his dismissal.

"the most ignorant man who had ever occupied the White House"—House Speaker Tip O'Neill. He also called Reagan "Herbert Hoover with a smile."

"his brains are negligible"—Henry Kissinger, on the Nixon White House tapes.

a man of *"limited mental capacity"*—Richard Nixon, on the same tapes.

"dumb"—Garry Wills, in 1980. Writing about Reagan's misstatements on the stump, Wills said, "It's not senility that makes him dumb. Hollywood did that a long time ago."

Running against him in the 1980 primaries, George H. W. Bush called Reagan's plans, based on the idea that lowering tax rates would increase tax revenues, *"economic madness"* and *"voodoo economics."*

His *"life seems to be governed by a few anecdotes and vignettes that he has memorized"*— Jimmy Carter, in his diary.

"Poor dear, there's nothing between his ears"—British prime minister Margaret Thatcher.

"a useful idiot for Soviet propaganda"—Howard Phillips of the Conservative Caucus, objecting to Reagan's plan to sign an arms reduction treaty. Phillips also called Reagan "a weak man with a strong wife" and the "speech reader-in-chief" for appeasers.

"neither fox nor hedgehog. He was as dumb as a stump."—journalist Christopher Hitchens.

"a triumph of the embalmer's art"—writer Gore Vidal.

The Wimp Factor (George H. W. Bush, 1989–1993)

Reagan's vice president, George H. W. Bush, won the presidency in 1988 after a hard-fought Republican primary. Reagan himself remained neutral until the nomination was decided and at one point was quoted in the *Washington Post* as telling friends that Bush "doesn't seem to stand for anything." Reagan denied making the comment.

"a pin-stripin' polo-playin' umbrella-totin' Ivy Leaguer"

Having served in the House of Representatives, as UN ambassador, as ambassador to China, and as CIA director, Bush was from the fading Eastern establishment wing of the GOP, with a Yale education, service in World War II, a career as a transplanted Texas oilman, and a combination of noblesse oblige and political ambition.

In Texas, he was seen as too patrician, too Yankee, and too preppy, leading to the characterization, attributed to Ohio governor Jim Rhodes, that "George Bush is the only guy I know who gets out of the shower to take a piss." Bush also had a reputation for changing his positions as he tried to balance his own middle-of-the-road instincts with those of his Texas constituents—and later to conform to Reagan's views. He came to suffer from what *Newsweek* magazine called "the Wimp Factor" in its October 19, 1987, issue. The characterization would stick, but Bush managed a deft bit of image judo in 1988, successfully tagging his Democratic opponent Michael Dukakis with the image of softness.

Bush's single term saw successful diplomatic and military operations in Panama and the Middle East and a new relationship with the Soviet Union after the fall of the Berlin Wall, but his presidency came to be plagued by a recession. He was challenged from the right in his own party by Patrick Buchanan, a former Nixon speechwriter turned television commentator, and in the 1992 general election Bush was perceived not so much as wimpy but as out of touch with economic issues. No amount of image judo would suffice to save him.

SAID OF

George H. W. Bush

"a carpetbagger from Connecticut who is drilling oil for the Sheik of Kuwait"—Texas senator Ralph Yarborough, in 1964 when Bush ran against him.

"born with a silver foot in his mouth"—Texas state treasurer Ann Richards, keynoting the 1988 Democratic National Convention, blending the two figures of speech "foot in the mouth" and "born with a silver spoon in the mouth."

"a spoon-fed little rich kid"—William Loeb, who also called Bush "a wimp."

"a pin-stripin' polo-playin' umbrella-totin' Ivy Leaguer, born with a silver spoon so far back in his mouth that you couldn't get it out with a crowbar"—Alabama attorney general Bill Baxley.

"I'll get you some day, you fucking Nazi"—a whispered aside from Republican senator Bob Dole to Bush after the 1980 New Hampshire debate. Reagan and Bush had agreed to a two-person debate, but at the last minute Reagan proposed to open it to all the candidates. When the candidates were invited on stage, Bush objected that he preferred to "play by the rules" originally agreed on.

"a man who freezes under pressure"—Reagan to an adviser, after the 1980 New Hampshire debate.

Bush *"placed his manhood in a blind trust"* to be Reagan's running mate—Garry Trudeau's *Doonesbury*.

"silly and effeminate"—Jimmy Carter.

"Bush will be a eunuch on his honeymoon"—columnist Fred Barnes, writing in the *New Republic*.

"King George"—Patrick Buchanan, after winning the 1992 New Hampshire primary.

"a Pekingese curled around the ankles of China's tyrants"—columnist George F. Will. Will also referred to Bush as "a lapdog" and to his presidency as "lighter than air."

"You'd think he was running for First Lady instead of for president"—Bill Clinton in 1992, referring to Bush campaign attacks on Hillary Clinton.

Wimping Out

By 1988, *wimp* was firmly established in American usage, but its origins remain mysterious.

The *OED* defines the word as "a feeble or ineffectual person; one who is spineless" and provides a 1920 citation from George Ade, who refers to a "dejected wimp." The *OED* suggests a possible connection to *whimper*, but it also gives a second entry for *wimp* as British slang for "a woman or girl," which may be "an abbreviated corruption of *women*."

A 1919 article by W. T. McAtee in *The Railway Conductor* suggested that *wimp* arose in the context of World War I, along with *pacifist, conscientious objector*, and *slacker*. McAtee quotes an army officer who defined a *wimp* as a faux idealist who signs up to fight but "never exposes himself to any danger." The officer added, "The wimp . . . has a gleaming streak of 'yaller' in his hide which runs down to his backbone."

A few years later, newspaper readers met J. Wellington Wimpy, the foil in the *Popeye* comic strip, launched in 1934. Wimpy was a pudgy pseudo-intellectual who would "gladly pay you Tuesday for a hamburger today."

By the 1960s *wimp* re-emerged as college slang. A 1964 *American Speech* article by Lawrence Poston reported that *wimp* was "still mysterious and undefined" in his notes. Two years later, in "Notes on Campus Vocabulary," Poston and Francis Stillman were more definitive, glossing it as "someone who is offensive in a negative, passive, wishy-washy manner."

They point to use of the adjective *wimpish* in Sinclair Lewis's *Arrowsmith*, which has "'Casper Milquetoast' overtones." Around the same time, the University of South Dakota's publication *Current Slang* gave the definition of *wimp* as "a backward person," with the citation, "He's a real wimp on a date."

George H. W. Bush, by the way, was not the first president to be dubbed a *wimp*. That distinction goes to Jimmy Carter, whose economic plan was dubbed "Mush from the Wimp" in the headline of an editorial in the March 15, 1980, *Boston Globe*. The headline was a *Globe* editor's in-house joke that inadvertently made it into print in the first edition of the paper before being corrected.

Slick Willy (Bill Clinton, 1993–2001)

Bill Clinton represented a changing of the generations. The first baby-boomer president, Clinton was a four-time governor of Arkansas, a former Rhodes Scholar, and a Yale Law School graduate. He was given the nickname "Slick Willy" in Arkansas, a description bestowed by

> "a nerdy little flower-child peacenik"

Paul Greenberg of the *Arkansas Democrat Gazette*, which won out over "Kid Clinton," "Boy Governor," and "Young Smoothie." In the three-way 1992 contest with incumbent Bush and third-party candidate Ross Perot, Clinton won with 43 percent of the popular vote.

Many of Clinton's setbacks over his two terms were of his own making. Clinton's penchant for verbal hair-splitting was evident in the 1992 campaign as he attempted to finesse questions about his Vietnam draft status, his relationship with actress Gennifer Flowers, and his marijuana use. These led the *New York Times* in its backhanded endorsement to say, "He has, when pressed, shown a discomfiting tendency to blur truthful clarity."

Clinton's presidency was a roller coaster. In the 1994 mid-term elections, Republicans gained fifty-four seats in the House of Representatives and eight seats in the Senate. Yet the Republican "Contract with America" foundered, and in 1996 Clinton prevailed in another three-way race. Clinton's second term was largely consumed by a sex scandal involving intern Monica Lewinsky and an impeachment trial for perjury. Nevertheless, Clinton left office with approval ratings matching Ronald Reagan's.

Charges about Clinton's financial dealings were reiterated by right-wing media celebrities such as Rush Limbaugh, no longer constrained by the FCC fairness doctrine. And as early as 1994, a video appeared called *The Clinton Chronicles*. Subtitled "Investigation into the Alleged Criminal Activities of Bill Clinton," the video included comments from a man convinced that "Bill Clinton had my father killed to save his political career." Clinton privately seethed at attacks and at one point early in his presidency had a White House staffer compile a 332-page report about the spread of fringe stories from online media to the mainstream. That report, titled "Communication Stream of Conspiracy Commerce," became the basis for Hillary Clinton's 1998 claim of a vast right-wing conspiracy.

 SAID OF

Clinton

"I read reports of Bill Clinton's economic plan. You know something, I think he did inhale"—Kay Bailey Hutchison, then Texas state treasurer, referring to Clinton's claim that he smoked marijuana but didn't inhale.

a *"nerdy little flower-child peacenik demonstrating against his country"*—California Republican Robert Dornan in 1992.

"a draft-dodging, pro-gay greenhorn, married to a radical feminist"—Patrick Buchanan.

"bozos"—George H. W. Bush, referring to Clinton and Al Gore. During the 1992 campaign, Bush also referred to Clinton as "Waffle Man," "dodging the draft," and "slippery when wet." Later the two became famous friends.

"a Communist"—Representative Sonny Bono.

a *"spoiled brat" whose election proved that "the country has finally gone to hell"*—Richard Nixon, according to a memoir by Monica Crowley, his foreign policy assistant in the 1990s.

"the enemy of normal Americans"—House Speaker Newt Gingrich, referring to Clinton's administration. In 1994 Gingrich circulated a memo encouraging Republicans to use words such as "sick," "pathetic," "traitor," "corrupt," "illegitimate," and "criminal" when referring to the Clinton administration.

"a bore"—legendary broadcaster David Brinkley, on an open mic immediately after Clinton's re-election.

"the big creep"—Monica Lewinsky, on a secret recording made by confidante Linda Tripp.

"a slut"—car alarm magnate Darrell Issa, running for the Senate in 1998. Issa attributed the comment to his wife.

a *"scumbag"*—Dan Burton, chairman of the House Government Reform and Oversight Committee.

"President Caligula"—Oliver North, one-time deputy director of the National Security Council turned commentator.

"debauched, debased, and defamed"—televangelist Pat Robertson.

"a murderer"—commentator/comedian Norm MacDonald, on a 2000 episode of *The View*, in an apparently joking reference to the conspiracy theories about Clinton having people killed.

"a predator president with a wife who enabled him"—former New York mayor Rudolph Giuliani, in 2016, defending Donald Trump by attacking Clinton.

Shrub (George W. Bush, 2001–2009)

George W. Bush grew up in Midland, Texas, and followed his father's path into the Texas oil business and later into politics, making an unsuccessful run for Congress in 1978. In 1994, Bush challenged the incumbent governor Ann Richards, winning an upset victory. In 2000,

> "a playground bully cleaned up for church"

he battled Vice President Al Gore to a photo-finish in the election for the presidency. Florida's crucial electoral college votes remained undecided until the Supreme Court weighed in, 5-4, in the case *Bush v. Gore.*

Bush's perceived penchant for misspeaking became a feature of the election and his presidency when humorists began referring to his malapropisms and verbal slips as Bushisms. During the 2000 campaign he told an Arkansas audience that critics had "misunderestimated" him and another group in New Hampshire that "I know how hard it is for you to put food on your family." As a candidate, he was also mocked as a "playground bully cleaned up for church," and one Republican governor referred to him as "the only guy in history who had to take lessons to get that smirk off his face."

Bush faced challenges abroad and domestically, most notably the terrorist attacks of September 11, 2001, and the later wars in Afghanistan and Iraq, which began in 2001 and 2003. In his second term, Bush became known for the government's lackluster response to Hurricane Katrina and for the Great Recession of 2007–2008. Bush left office in 2009 with a 22 percent approval rating.

As president and afterward, Bush rarely responded to insults and criticism. In one interview, with Argentine journalist Enrique Gratas, Bush commented, "I've been in politics a long time. I've always found the best thing is to do is to do what you think is right and move beyond the name-calling."

After leaving office, Bush commented that the insult that stung the most was from rapper Kanye West, who implied he was a racist for his response to Hurricane Katrina. In his memoir, Bush wrote that "I faced a lot of criticism as president. I didn't like hearing people claim that I lied about Iraq's weapons of mass destruction or cut taxes to benefit the rich. But the suggestion that I was racist because of the response to Katrina represented an all-time low." West later relented, saying that he "didn't have the grounds to call him a racist" and that people "don't always choose the right words." Bush told a television interviewer that he appreciated West's comments, adding, "I'm not a hater, I didn't hate Conway West," mispronouncing the name. He later got Kanye's name right.

 SAID OF

George W. Bush

"Shrub"—Texas journalist Molly Ivins, making wordplay with the Bush name.

a *"party frat-boy type"*—Marilyn Quayle, wife of former vice president Dan Quayle.

"obviously dyslexic, and dyslexic to the point of near-illiteracy"— Christopher Hitchens, in the *Nation*.

"an empty suit, meaner than his dad"—Bill Clinton, as reported by historian Taylor Branch.

a *"fake cowboy"*—the *Village Voice.*

"a chest beater in a borrowed flight suit, instructing us to max out our credit cards for the cause"—writer Susan Faludi, commenting on his leadership in the war on terror.

"the monkey in the middle"—journalist Erin Burnett, commenting on video of Bush with other nations' leaders.

a *"feckless blood-spattered plutocrat"*—playwright Tony Kushner.

a *"treacherous little freak"*—writer Hunter S. Thompson.

a *"high-functioning moron"*—Democratic consultant/commentator Paul Begala.

"a chicken hawk"—Paul Hackett, a 2004 Democratic congressional candidate in Ohio. Hackett also called Bush "a son-of-a-bitch."

"a deserter"—filmmaker Michael Moore, regarding Bush's National Guard service.

"I think this guy is a loser"—Senate majority leader Harry Reid, in 2005, speaking to high schoolers.

Barack Who? (Barack Obama, 2009–2017)

The recession of 2007 opened a path to the presidency for a relatively unknown Illinois senator by the name of Barack Hussein Obama II. Representing a new generation, Obama won the Democratic nomination in a large field of competitors, the most persistent of whom was Senator Hillary Clinton. Obama's eventual Republican opponent, Arizona senator John McCain, was unable to overcome the drag of the

> "a dirty capitalist like the rest of us"

economic crisis and the unpopular war in Iraq, and Obama, by contrast, projected inclusiveness, calm, and "hope."

Economic recovery was slow, and with the rise of the anti-tax Tea Party movement and the vitriol accompanying healthcare reform, the Republicans made significant gains in the 2010 election, which would check Obama's agenda for the remainder of his term.

Race played a role in much of the invective aimed at Obama, amplified by the echo chamber of social media. Social media use grew from just 10 percent of the US population in 2008 to nearly 80 percent in 2016, providing a landscape for the viral replication of insulting commentary and images. Insults no longer needed to be spoken or written—they could simply be shared or liked. The so-called birther conspiracy added another level. Those attempting to delegitimize Obama's election would claim that Obama "has yet to have to prove that he's a citizen," as Rush Limbaugh put it.

Sometimes the birther rhetoric incorporated overtly racist memes, such as the e-mail sent by Marilyn Davenport, a California Republican Party official, which had Obama's face superimposed onto a baby chimpanzee, with two chimp parents and the tagline, "Now you know why—No birth certificate." Obama's international background also entered into insults. Former House Speaker Newt Gingrich suggested that Obama might have a "Kenyan, anti-colonial" worldview, attributing the idea to commentator Dinesh D'Souza. Obama detractors would invoke race with such code words as "affirmative action candidate" (Rush Limbaugh) and "food stamp president" (Newt Gingrich).

Obama was attacked as being antiwhite (conservative commentator Glenn Beck said, "This guy is, I believe, a racist"). But he was also attacked as not being black enough and for "acting like he's white," as Jesse Jackson put it. Rumors also circulated about Obama's religion, and one heckler at an Obama event in 2011 shouted out "Barack Obama is the anti-Christ."

Beyond this othering by race and background, Obama was insulted as professorial, elitist, and boring. Meghan McCain, the daughter of Senator John McCain, remarked that she "would pay money not to have to sit through a speech from President Obama because I find him that boring. It's like sitting through every class I hated in college." Former Pennsylvania senator Rick Santorum, commenting on Obama's education initiatives, took him to task this way: "President Obama once said he wants everybody in America to go to college. What a snob."

 SAID OF

Obama

"Barack Obama: Born of the corrupt Chicago political machine"—2008 McCain television ad.

"He is unhinged"—Fox commentator Sean Hannity.

"kind of a wuss"—conservative commentator Tucker Carlson.

"This guy is such a total pussy, it's stunning"—Fox News military analyst Ralph Peters.

a *"food stamp president"*—Newt Gingrich.

a *"Kenyan creampuff"*—William Bradford, later a short-lived appointee in the Trump administration's Energy Department.

"a special kind of stupid"—former Alaska governor Sarah Palin.

a *"weak-kneed capitulator-in-chief"*—Palin.

"just another puppet"—hip-hop artist Black the Ripper.

"lazy"—Republican John Sununu, after the first Obama-Romney debate in 2012.

"a dirty capitalist like the rest of us"—Meghan McCain, referring to Obama's postpresidency speaking fees.

"the deporter-in-chief"—Janet Murguía, president of the National Council on La Raza, a Latino advocacy group.

a "moron"—former New York mayor Rudolph Giuliani.

"He is the founder of ISIS"—Donald Trump, who later claimed he was being sarcastic.

"a dictator"—former Maine governor Paul LePage.

"I thought he was kind of a dick yesterday"—commentator Mark Halperin on MSNBC, on Obama's press conference the day before.

Reality Show (Donald Trump, 2017–)

Like the election of 1980, the election of 2016 featured a pair of candidates with high disapproval ratings, Hillary Clinton and Donald J. Trump, with a result that surprised many pollsters. Trump, who began the race considered merely a publicity-seeking vanity candidate, lost the popular vote but won the electoral college.

> "the orange prince of American self-publicity"

The signature images of Trump's presidency thus far—investigations, staff chaos, and government by tweet—suggest disarray. Yet Trump's rhetoric, particularly with large crowds of enthusiastic supporters, can be surprisingly effective. His use of simple vocabulary and repetition, together with his ability to visually and verbally convey disgust, motivates his angry political base. His style, a reversal of the usual strategy of candidates' aiming to appear presidential, has been to go on the offensive with insults. In the 2016 primary season, Trump insulted his Republican opponents with nicknames such as "Mr. Meltdown" and "Lyin' Ted," and with characterizations of Jeb Bush as a "sad sack," "spoiled child," "lightweight," and "puppet." Former Hewlett Packard CEO Carly Fiorina's looks were mocked, with Trump commenting to a *Rolling Stone* reporter (when a video clip zoomed in on Fiorina), "Look at that face! Would anyone vote for that? Can you imagine that, the face of our next president?" Matters were even more heated in the general election campaign against Hillary Clinton. On television's *60 Minutes* in July 2016, Trump said, "Hillary Clinton is a liar," and he referred to her on the campaign trail as "Crooked Hillary," to audience chants of "Lock her up."

In the early fall of 2016, Trump and Clinton held three debates, in New York, Missouri, and Nevada. In the first, Trump alluded to Clinton's appearance and health, saying, "She doesn't have the look." In the second, Trump said Clinton had "tremendous hate in her heart" and promised that she would "be in jail" when he was president. Trump also referred to Clinton as "the devil." In the third debate, on foreign policy, Clinton remarked that Russian president Vladimir Putin preferred Trump because he wanted to "have a puppet as president of the United States." In the exchange that followed Trump exclaimed, "You're the puppet!" And when Clinton jabbed at Trump about paying taxes, he interjected, "Such a nasty woman."

Donald Trump uses insults as his primary means of expression, referring to members of his own administration as "weak" and "dumb" and to political adversaries as "crazy." Especially troubling to many has been the ways he insults and attacks the news media as "enemies of the American people," "truly the opposition party," "corrupt," "unpatriotic," "troublemakers," and purveyors of "fake news," even going so far as to suggest changing the libel laws and revoking licenses. In one 2017 tweet, he wrote, "Network news has become so partisan, distorted and fake that licenses must be challenged and, if appropriate, revoked."

In part, such harshness is a continuation of the media shifts in the 1990s, evident in the invective aimed at Bill Clinton, George W. Bush, and Barack Obama, and amplified by the rise of social media. However, the national tone is also set by the persona and personality of the president, and Donald Trump is both a symptom and a carrier of national incivility. Some have suggested that his insults and tweets are a deliberate strategy to distract the public from other news or policy initiatives. Others see them as an indication of an erratic, vindictive personality. Whether a rhetorical tactic or personality trait, Trump's means of responding to challenges and interacting with others is to assail with contempt. The *New York Times* has listed 567 people, places, or things that Trump has insulted as of January 2019.

Donald Trump's behavior, in turn, gives license to those who wish to express themselves in the same way. As early as 1988, publisher Graydon Carter, in a satirical ad in *Spy* magazine, referred to Trump as "a short-fingered vulgarian"; by bringing vulgarity to the mainstream, Donald Trump has himself become a magnet for invective mocking his appearance, behavior, temperament, and performance. British politician Marcus Fysh called him "the orange prince of American self-publicity," referring to his tan, and he has been mocked as "President Cheeto." Members of his own party and administration have referred to him as "a jackass," "an asshole," "a fucking moron," and "a little wet noodle." In 2019

Rashida Tlaib, a newly elected member of Congress, publicly called him a "motherfucker."

Insults have always been a part of American politics. At the moment, they are center stage and show little sign of abating.

 SAID OF

Trump

"a thirteen-year-old"—former New Jersey governor Chris Christie, during the 2016 primary season.

"a sniveling coward," "a big, loud New York bully"—Texas senator Ted Cruz.

"a phony, a fraud," "a con artist"—Mitt Romney, Republican candidate for president in 2012, now a senator from Utah.

"a jackass"—Senator Lindsey Graham. Graham also called Trump a "kook," "a race-baiting bigot," and "the most flawed nominee in the history of the Republican Party."

"a malignant clown—unprepared and unfit to be president of the United States"—Mark Kirk, Republican senator, while running for re-election in 2016.

a *"jagoff"*—businessman Mark Cuban, using a homegrown Pittsburgh insult.

a *"fascist, loofa-faced shit-gibbon"*—Pennsylvania state senator Daylin Leach, tweeting.

"Our unhinged president"—Robert Reich. According to journalist Bob Woodward, Chief of Staff John Kelly also referred to Trump as "unhinged" and as an "idiot."

"an asshole, but he's our asshole"—California Republican congressman Duncan Hunter in 2017.

a *"fucking moron"*—Rex Tillerson during his tenure as Trump's secretary of state.

"Trump Is Woody Allen Without the Humor"—title of a 2017 *Wall Street Journal* article by former Reagan speechwriter Peggy Noonan. In the article, Noonan referred to Trump as "weak and sniveling" and as "a drama queen."

"Lazy Boy"—a 2017 *Newsweek* cover showing Trump in a recliner and describing him as "bored and tired."

"President Spanky"—Stephen Colbert on *The Late Show*, referring to porn star Stormy Daniels's account of spanking Trump with a copy of *Forbes* magazine.

"an economic traitor"—Boston University economist and *Forbes* magazine contributor Laurence Kotlikoff, commenting on the trade war strategy. *New York Times* columnist Charles Blow took it a step further, ending a column about the Helsinki meeting between Donald Trump and Vladimir Putin by writing: "Simply put, Trump is a traitor and may well be treasonous."

"a little wet noodle"—former California governor Arnold Schwarzenegger after the Helsinki meeting. Schwarzenegger said, in his bodybuilder persona, "President Trump, I just saw your press conference with President Putin and it was embarrassing. I mean, you stood there like a little wet noodle, like a little fanboy."

"the biggest wimp ever to serve as president"—Conservative commentator Ann Coulter, when Trump agreed to reopen the government in January 2019.

The Art of the Insult

Making insults can be an art form. Doing it well requires attention to the aesthetics of the genre and the communicative function of language.

An artful, well-crafted insult should do four things:

Capture the moment: Address what is on the minds of the audience. The characterizations of Benjamin Harrison as "human iceberg" and Woodrow Wilson as a "human icicle" got to the heart of their aloofness.

The mocking of Andrew Johnson as "Judas Johnson" similarly captured public perceptions of his character.

Be memorable: Employ images and phrasing that endure over time. When Congresswoman Patricia Schroeder tagged Ronald Reagan as "the Teflon-coated President," she created a lasting picture of his seeming imperviousness to criticism.

Be specific: Use complex enough language and metaphor to build insults involving both fact and interpretation. Harding's speeches were referred to as "an army of pompous phrases moving across the landscape in search of an idea," and the images of a wandering infantry of words painted a vivid picture of Harding's verbosity.

Embrace the poetry of language: Draw on double meaning, euphony, freshness, and surprise. Teddy Roosevelt's quip that Taft "no doubt means well, but he means well feebly" uses repetition to contrast intention and results. Hunter S. Thompson's reference to Nixon as "a swine of a man and a jabbering dupe of a president" likewise brings together parallel insults, the first setting up the second. Shorter bits of fresh language and wordplay are equally effective, such as the renaming of Rutherford Hayes as Rutherfraud or Clarence Darrow's characterization of Harding as a "human smudge."

A Catalog of Presidential Insults

I offer here a catalog of insults. Not every insult from the text is listed, but enough are to illustrate the main semantic categories used to insult presidents.

While many insults of course fit in more than a single category, there is a relatively small set of types, nouns and adjectives referring to intelligence, appearance, character, background, and behavior.

I have necessarily made judgment calls, sometimes lumping items together in categories and sometimes splitting them. And some insults are tricky. Tom Wolfe referred to Jimmy Carter as a "Missionary lectern-pounding Amen ten-finger C-major-chord Sister-Martha-at-the-Yamaha-keyboard loblolly piney-woods Baptist." How should this be characterized? I've grouped it under *Othering*, using that category for insults that attack by singling out difference: ethnic, racial, religious, and so on.

The listing is intended to serve as both a handy reference and a source for keywords and categories for further study.

Adultery and sex: the pimp, the panderer (John Quincy Adams), adulterer (Jackson), rake, libertine, a moral leper, a coarse debauchee (Cleveland), a he-harlot (Harding), debauched, debased, and defamed, a slut, a predator president (Clinton), President Spanky (Trump).

Animals: the fireside Hyena of character (Jackson), a crawling reptile (Van Buren), a gorilla, a baboon (Lincoln), an angle-worm (Garfield), a stalled ox (Arthur), a white-livered cur, a sad jellyfish (McKinley), the golf pig (Taft), a dead whale on a beach (Eisenhower), a petrified pig (Reagan), a Pekingese, a lapdog (George H. W. Bush), the monkey in the middle (George W. Bush), baby chimp (Obama), a shit-gibbon (Trump).

Arrogant, aggressive, bullying, quarrelsome, violent: perverse and mulish (John Quincy Adams), bloodthirsty, vindictive, a monster, a bully (Jackson), the great presidential quarreler (Grant), arrogant and obstinate (Cleveland), obstinate and pug-nacious (Benjamin Harrison), that wild man, a dangerous and ominous jingo (Theodore Roosevelt), a bully with an Air Force (Lyndon Johnson), an arrogant political bully (Ford), a play-ground bully cleaned up for church (George W. Bush), a big, loud New York bully (Trump).

Asshole. *See* Invective.

Bores: an oratorical mortician (Carter), a bore (Clinton), boring (Obama).

Clown: clownish (John Quincy Adams), a low, cunning clown (Lincoln), this insolent clownish creature (Andrew Johnson), catastrophically close to making himself into a national clown

(Ford), bozos (Bill Clinton and Al Gore), a clown (Obama), a malignant clown (Trump).

Cold, cold-blooded: secret, sly, selfish, cold, calculating, distrustful, treacherous (Van Buren), surly, cold and indifferent (Grant), the human iceberg, cold-blooded (Benjamin Harrison), a human icicle (Wilson).

Comparisons: a greater tyrant than Cromwell, Caesar, or Bonaparte (Jackson), as opposite to Jackson as dung is to a diamond (Van Buren), if Andy Johnson was a snake, he would hide in the grass and bite the heels of rich men's children (Andrew Johnson), a scientific Goth resembling Alaric, destroying the country as he goes (Grant), as glacial as a Siberian stripped of his furs (Benjamin Harrison), better fitted to be a scullion at Delmonico's than in the White House (Arthur), no more backbone than a chocolate éclair (McKinley), to call Mr. Wilson a weathercock is unfair to weathercocks (Wilson), more wicked than Hitler (Kennedy), der Fuehrer (Lyndon Johnson), Eisenhower without medals, worse than Harding and Hoover put together (Ford), a Southern-fried McGovern, a Reagan clone (Carter), Herbert Hoover with a smile (Reagan), a eunuch on his honeymoon (George H. W. Bush), Woody Allen without the humor (Trump).

Cowards: a dastardly poltroon (Jefferson), a red petticoat general (William Henry Harrison), a coward, hiding behind his office (Polk), cowardly (Fillmore), wholly without moral courage (Pierce), a coward (Buchanan), has no will, no courage, no executive capacity (Lincoln), a coward and an ingrate (Arthur), a coward, a yellow belly (Wilson), a spineless sort of individual (Harding), a coward (Eisenhower), a feckless blood-spattered plutocrat, a chicken hawk (George W. Bush).

Criminals: an assassin (Washington), a murderer (Jackson, Pierce, Clinton), a robber-chief (Polk), not only a liar, but a false swearer and a bribe-taker (Garfield). *See also* Traitors.

Demagogues: a demagogue (Jefferson), a bold, unscrupulous, and vindictive demagogue (Van Buren), an unprincipled dema-gogue (Andrew Johnson), a demagogue and flatterer (Theodore Roosevelt), a demagogue (Nixon).

Dictators, despots: as despotic as the Grand Turk (Jefferson), despotic (Fillmore), a military autocrat, a brainless tyrant (Lincoln), our president-czar (Garfield), a besotted tyrant (Cleveland), cold-blooded and despotic (Benjamin Harrison), usurper or dictator (Wilson), a tyrant who happens temporarily to be president of the United States (Hoover).

Disability. *See* Othering.

Dotards. *See* Old.

Draft dodger: a draft-dodging, pro-gay greenhorn (Clinton), a deserter (George W. Bush).

Dumb: old muttonhead (Washington), one of the most egre-gious fools on the continent (John Adams), a mind neither rapid nor rich (Monroe), a barbarian who could not write a sentence of grammar (Jackson), an imbecile (Tyler), an illiterate frontier colonel (Taylor), an imbecile (Buchanan), an idiot, illiterate, an imbecile president (Lincoln), uniquely stupid, [stupid] enough to upset Darwin (Grant), not a ray of force or intellect (Hayes), not broad enough in mental equipment, a flathead (Arthur), a plodding mind, limited knowledge, and narrow capacities (Cleveland), a fathead, a puzzlewit (Taft), bungalow-minded, the only man, woman or child who wrote a simple declarative sentence with seven grammatical errors (Harding), an economic ignoramus, a gibbering idiot, ignorant (Franklin Roosevelt), an economic ignoramus (Kennedy), a dumb bastard (Ford), a complete birdbrain (Carter), the most ignorant man who had ever occupied the White House, dumb as a stump (Reagan), a high-functioning moron (George W. Bush), a special kind of stupid, a moron (Obama), a fucking moron (Trump).

Drunkards: brandy-soaked (Jefferson), a hero of many a well-fought bottle (Pierce), the sot, the drunken tailor (Andrew Johnson), a drunkard (Grant), a drunk (Teddy Roosevelt), our drunken friend (Nixon).

Elitists: a stinking little aristocrat (Benjamin Harrison), a rainy-day plutocrat (Franklin Roosevelt), the enemy of normal Americans (Clinton), a snob (Obama). *See also* Pedants.

Fake, liar, charlatan, con man, hypocrite: a hypocrite, an impostor (Washington), a dissembling patriot, a contemptible hypocrite (Jefferson), an old lying scamp (John Quincy Adams), a confidence man (Jackson), mendacious (Polk), a facetious pettifogger (Lincoln), a clever trickster (Garfield), the greatest fakir of all times, a charlatan, a mountebank, a honeyfuggler, a thimblerigger (Theodore Roosevelt), an unctuous charlatan, a liar and an ingrate (Wilson), a big liar (Hoover), a Quack, a great betrayer and liar, a chameleon on plaid, a liar and a fake, a prize honeyfuggler (Franklin Roosevelt), a stinking hypocrite (Eisenhower), a liar, Bullshit Johnson (Lyndon Johnson), a no-good lying bastard (Nixon), a goddamn liar, a smiling hypocrite, a phony, a user of political snake oil (Carter), a con man (Clinton), a fake cowboy (George W. Bush), authentically dishonest (Obama), a pathological liar, a con artist (Trump).

Funny looking. *See* Reference to physical appearance.

Gendered insults: hideous hermaphroditical character (John Adams), evidently to want manly firmness (Madison), a wife-made man (Fillmore), Miss Nancy, a miserable gabbling old granny (Buchanan), Granny Hayes, Queen Victoria in breeches (Hayes), Jane Dandy (Theodore Roosevelt), effeminate, neither a gentleman nor a real man (Wilson), not a man's man (Kennedy), a wimp, silly and effeminate (George H. W. Bush), a wuss, a pussy (Obama), a drama queen (Trump).

Immoral: a slur upon the moral government of the world (Jefferson), wicked (Lincoln), devoid of patriotism and principle (Grant), dishonorable (Wilson). *See also* Adultery and sex.

Incompetent, ineffective: unfit (John Adams), wholly unfit for the storms of War (Madison), a bloated mass of political putridity (Buchanan), universally an admitted failure, this presidential pigmy (Lincoln), the most formidable disaster that has befallen the country since the Civil War (Theodore Roosevelt), a blunderer (Taft), an utter incompetent (Franklin Roosevelt), the big fool (Lyndon Johnson), a disaster (Carter), a loser (George W. Bush).

Indecisive. *See* Weak and indecisive.

Invective (including SOBs, assholes, jackasses, deviants, etc.): damned infernal old scoundrel (Monroe), an arch scoundrel, the prince of villains (Van Buren), the Executive Ass (Tyler), a scoundrel (Hayes), a base fellow (Garfield), the enemy of the good people (McKinley), that damned cowboy, a freak (Theodore Roosevelt), a prime jackass (Wilson), a slob, a human smudge (Harding), a son-of-a-bitch (Hoover), a scab president (Franklin Roosevelt), a son-of-a-bitch, a monster, a nincompoop, a little bastard (Truman), a yellow son-of-a-bitch, that old asshole (Eisenhower), damned son-of-a-bitch, that bastard (Lyndon Johnson), a no good lying bastard, a filthy lying son-of-a-bitch, a shit (Nixon), a jerk (Ford), a little schmuck (Carter), a fucking Nazi (George H. W. Bush), a scumbag (Clinton), a son-of-a-bitch (George W. Bush), kind of a dick (Obama), an asshole, a motherfucker (Trump).

Lazy. *See* Temperament.

Looks. *See* Reference to physical appearance.

Old: a credulous, blind, dotard, old man (Jackson), a superannuated old woman, a pitiable dotard (William Henry Harrison), the most amazing of fossils (Buchanan), a tired old man (Franklin

Roosevelt), a triumph of the embalmer's art (Reagan), a dotard (Trump).

Othering: a confirmed infidel, a howling atheist (Jefferson), a cannibal (Jackson), inhuman and irreligious (Lincoln), alien enemy, citizen of a foreign state, the great apostate, white trash (Andrew Johnson), a usurper with a disturbed mind (Hayes), clearly insane (Theodore Roosevelt), a recent acquisition to our population (Hoover), that crippled son-of-a-bitch (Franklin Roosevelt), a goddamn Mick, a little scrawny fellow with rickets (Kennedy), a white honky character, Dr. Cornpone (Lyndon Johnson), a carpetbagger (George H. W. Bush), dyslexic to the point of near-illiteracy (George W. Bush), a Kenyan creampuff (Obama).

Pedants: repulsive pedant (John Adams), a pedagogue (John Quincy Adams), a trained elocutionist, a strutting pedagogue (Wilson).

Puppets, tool, stooge: a mere puppet or cypher, Napoleon's humble imitator and submissive satellite (Madison), a fawning parasite, a mere tool in the hands of the French (Monroe), a tool of Jackson (Polk), a dupe (Pierce), a baby politician (Grant), Conkling's man Friday (Arthur), Mark Hanna's echo (McKinley), the servile functionary of the trusts, the bellhop of Wall Street (Theodore Roosevelt), an errand boy for the capitalistic system (Coolidge), a Wall Street tool (Franklin Roosevelt), Pendergast's bellhop (Truman), a stooge for Wall Street (Eisenhower), just another puppet (Obama), Putin's puppet (Trump).

Reference to physical appearance: hoary headed, old, querulous, bald, blind, crippled, toothless (John Adams), a withered apple John (Madison), hatchet-faced, horrid looking (Lincoln), fat (Cleveland, Taft, Hoover), a moosejaw (Franklin Roosevelt), a good-looking mortician (Eisenhower), a pretty boy (Kennedy), a Peewee (Nixon), the orange prince of American self-publicity, loofa-faced (Trump).

Reference to race, religion, ethnicity, gender, origins. *See* Othering.

Second-raters (third-raters, and the like): a book politician (Madison), a blighted burr (Polk), of very ordinary capacity (Taylor), a small neighborhood candidate (Fillmore), a kind of third-rate county, or, at most, state politician (Pierce), a third-rate Western lawyer (Lincoln), a third-rate nonentity (Hayes), about the last man who would be considered eligible (Arthur), a flubdub with a streak of the second-rate (Taft), a respectable Ohio politician of the second class, a cheese-paring of a man (Harding), probably the man of smallest caliber who has ever been made president of the United States (Coolidge), without any important qualifications (Franklin Roosevelt), a nice old gentleman in a golf cart (Eisenhower), a triumph of lowest-common-denominator politics, a fine-looking man in a Lake Wobegon sort of way (Ford), the failed governor of a small state (Clinton), an empty suit (George W. Bush).

Spoiled: momma's boy (Franklin Roosevelt), Papa's pet, spoiled (Kennedy), a spoon-fed little rich kid (George H. W. Bush), a spoiled brat (Clinton).

Temperament: mean, wedded to authority, order, and pomp (Washington), indolent, dilatory, temporizing, timorous, poisoned with Ambition (Jefferson), bland and accommodating (Arthur), simply big, fat, and lazy (Taft), cheap (Coolidge), a thin-lipped hater (Truman), mean, abusive, and very unstable (Lyndon Johnson), a cheap bastard (Nixon), governed by a few anecdotes and vignettes that he has memorized (Reagan), the only guy in history who had to take lessons to get that smirk off his face, meaner than his dad (George W. Bush), lazy (Obama), Lazy Boy (Trump).

Traitor (including bits of hyperbole aimed at traitors to party or principle): a traitor (John Quincy Adams), mad, weak & a traitor [to the Whigs] (Tyler), an arch traitor (Pierce), as truly a traitor as was Benedict Arnold, the chief of the traitors (Buchanan), a Copperhead (Pierce, Buchanan), that renegade and traitor (Andrew Johnson), Judas Johnson (Andrew Johnson and Lyndon Johnson), a damned traitor (Cleveland), a traitor to his class (Franklin Roosevelt), a traitor (Truman, Kennedy, Lyndon Johnson, Trump), Wanted for Treason (fliers picturing Kennedy, and much later, Obama), a southern Benedict Arnold (Lyndon Johnson), an economic traitor (Trump).

Ugly. *See* Reference to physical appearance.

Usurper and accident: usurper (John Quincy Adams), His Accidency (Tyler), a second-hand president (Fillmore), a half-witted Usurper (Lincoln), the great accidental (Andrew Johnson), His Fraudulency, the Pretender (Hayes), a political accident (Truman), an interim president (Lyndon Johnson).

Vain, egotistical: vain and indiscreet (Harrison), weak & conceited (Tyler), a vain, showy, and pliant man (Pierce), vain as well as ill-tempered (Andrew Johnson), self-idolatrous (Cleveland), a dangerous egotist (Theodore Roosevelt), destined for a statue in a park, and . . . practicing the pose for it (McKinley), a megalomaniac (Franklin Roosevelt).

Violent. *See* Arrogant, aggressive, bullying, quarrelsome, violent.

Vulgar, coarse: coarse (John Quincy Adams), vulgar and vituperative, a vulgar village politician (Lincoln), coarse in his taste and blunt in his perceptions (Grant), a vulgar little Babbitt (Truman), a short-fingered vulgarian (Trump).

Weak and indecisive: pusillanimous (Washington), timid and indecisive (Madison), a weak man . . . made giddy with the idea of the Presidency (Taylor), the man of hesitation and doubt, irresolute and tranquil, timid (Fillmore), a doughface (Fillmore, Pierce, Buchanan), either the worst or the weakest of our presidents (Pierce), timid, vacillating & inefficient, wishy-washy, namby-pamby (Lincoln), a man of jelly, Mr. Face-both-ways, a jellyfish (McKinley), irresolute and easily frightened (Hoover), an incompetent wimp, a man who freezes under pressure (George H. W. Bush), a creampuff, weak-kneed capitulator-in-chief (Obama), weak and sniveling, a little wet noodle, a little fanboy, a wimp (Trump). *See also* Cowards.

Acknowledgments

This book began in a conversation with Oxford University Press editor Hallie Stebbins in January 2017. We were talking about a possible book project (not this one), and the topic of political insults came up. The upshot of that conversation was that a book on presidential insults needed to be written, and I agreed to sketch out a short proposal. The short proposal led to a longer one, a plan, and some sample material.

A couple of summers and many, many weekends later, this book emerged. I had always been interested in presidential history, and the project was an opportunity to revisit that long-held interest. And as a linguist, I have a professional interest in the history of words and how we use them.

No one writes in a vacuum, of course, and I am grateful to a number of people for suggestions, support, encouragement, sources, examples, and feedback: Daniel Alrick, Alma Rosa Alvarez, Robert Arellano, Tod Davies, Adam Davis, Bill Gholson, Merrilynne Lundahl, Diana Maltz, Margaret Perrow, Geoff Ridden, and Susan Walsh.

Special thanks to Anne Lobeck, Maureen Flanagan Battistella, Hallie Stebbins, Kristin Denham, Jeffrey Gayton, Michael

Niemann, Donald A. Ritchie, and a trio of anonymous OUP referees, who provided extensive and crucial feedback at various stages, and to Reilly Nycum, who helped prepare the index. Meredith Keffer's fine editorial hand helped me polish and hone the final manuscript. Morgan Pielli's fantastic artwork, simultaneously edgy and whimsical, gave *Dangerous Crooked Scoundrels* the proper finishing touches.

Kudos as well to the historians, journalists, and memoirists who documented so many of these events and comments. Their works have provided me with a reading list to dip back into for years to come and a sense of humility as a writer.

January 2019

ACKNOWLEDGMENTS

Sources and Bibliography

Most newspaper citations were found via newspapers.com or specific newspaper sites. The *New York Times* is abbreviated *NYT*, and the *Washington Post* as *WaPo*.

The Founders Online tool of the National Archives, hosted by the University of Virginia, http: //founders.archives.gov/, is abbreviated FO.

University presses are abbreviated UP.

The public domain image of John Trumbull's 1819 painting *The Declaration of Independence* was downloaded from the Wikimedia Commons, John Trumbull creator QS: P170,Q369263 (https: //commons.wikimedia.org/wiki/ File: Declaration_of_Independence_(1819),_by_John_Trumbull.jpg), "Declaration of Independence (1819), by John Trumbull", https: // creativecommons.org/licenses/by/4.0/legalcode.

Listed in the bibliography are books cited two or more times in the source notes. These are cited in the following source note listing using the author's last name and short title only. Other books are cited using full name, title, publisher, and date.

Chapter One
(Citations for insults discussed later in the text have not been included in this chapter's sources.)

"Thy tongue": *Cymbeline* (act III, scene IV).

"A modest man": *The Quote Investigator* (quoteinvestigator.com).

"writes fiction": *The Complete Works of Oscar Wilde*, Vol. IV, Oxford UP, 2007, 77.

"the gamut": *Oxford Dictionary of American Quotes*, Oxford UP, 2005, 340.

"In thy seat": *The Poetic Edda*, Vols. 1–2, Princeton UP, 1936, 157.

"I'm flying on": *Dumb It Down*, Universal, 2007.

"The president has not," "adult day care": "Donald Trump and Bob Corker: A timeline," CNN.com, Oct. 24, 2017.

"You lie!": "Rep. Wilson shouts, 'You lie' to Obama during speech," CNN.com, Sept. 10, 2009.

"Well, that hurts": "The Democratic debate in New Hampshire," *NYT*, Jan. 5, 2008.

"skunk's skunk's skunk": Cash, *Who the Hell Is William Loeb?*, xviii.

"economic ignoramus," "Pied Piper," "I just confine myself": Gardner, *Campaign Comedy*, 286.

"little bastard," "he is a man": Sachar, Abram, *The Course of Our Times*, Knopf, 1972, 407.

"Crooked Hillary": "At Florida rally, Trump resumes attacking 'Crooked Hillary Clinton,'" *WaPo*, Sept. 27, 2016.

"dyslexic": Hitchens, Christopher, "Why Dubya can't read," *The Nation*, Sept. 4, 2004.

Chapter Two

George Washington (1732–1799; in Office 1789–1797)

"could not write a sentence": Letter from Adams to Benjamin Rush, Nov. 11, 1807, FO.

"pusillanimity" and other quotes are from Paine's letter to George Washington, Thomas Paine National Historical Association, thomaspaine.org.

"Anglican, monarchical," "It would give you a fever": Jefferson, Thomas, *The Papers of Thomas Jefferson*, Vol. 29, *1 March 1796 to 31 December 1797*, Princeton UP, 2002, 73–88.

"forerunner": Burns, James M., and Susan Dunn, *George Washington*, Times Books, 2013, 289.

"loathings": Sheppard, *The Partisan Press*, 32.

"arrows of malevolence," "outrages": Letter from George Washington to Henry Lee, July 21, 1793, FO.

"l'assassin": Chernow, *Washington*, 768–769; The *Aurora*, March 11, 1897.

"weak general": Russell, Preston, "The Conway cabal," *American Heritage* 46, no. 1 (1995): 84–91.

"old muttonhead": Chernow, *Hamilton*, 520.

"bashaw": McCullough, *John Adams*, 464.

"most miserable politician": Tagg, *Benjamin Franklin Bache*, 278.

"The American nation has been debauched": Tagg, *Benjamin Franklin Bache*, 282.

"His mind was great": Letter from Jefferson to Dr. Walter Jones, Jan. 2, 1814, FO.

John Adams (1735–1826; in Office 1797–1801)

"sesquipadelity": McCullough, *John Adams*, 462.

"His Rotundity": Ellis, Joseph, *Founding Brothers: The Revolutionary Generation*, Knopf, 2013, 168.

"unbounded thirst": *The Life of Representative Matthew Lyon of Vermont and Kentucky*, http://history.house.gov/Historical-Highlights/1800-1850/The-life-of-Representative-Matthew-Lyon-of-Vermont-and-Kentucky/.

"old, querulous": Sheppard, *The Partisan Press*, 33.

"repulsive pedant," "hideous hermaphroditical": Callender, *The Prospect Before Us*, 1800.

"ordinary man" and other quotes: "A letter from Alexander Hamilton," FO.

"devoid of every moral purpose": Chernow, *Hamilton*, 613.

"bastard brat": Letter to Benjamin Rush, Jan. 25, 1806, FO.

"hoary-headed," "gross hypocrite," "one of the most," "strange": Callender, *The Prospect Before Us*.

"inferior": "A letter from Alexander Hamilton," FO.

"power-mad despot": Novotny, Patrick, *The Press in American Politics, 1787–2012*, ABC-CLIO, 2014, 19.

"vain, irritable": Letter from Jefferson to Madison, Jan. 30, 1787, FO.

"out of his senses": Chernow, *Hamilton*, 518.

"insane message": Ferling, John, *Jefferson and Hamilton: The Rivalry That Forged a Nation*, Bloomsbury, 2013, 354.

Thomas Jefferson (1743–1826; in Office 1801–1809)

"indolent": Letter from Adams to Abigail, Dec. 26, 1793, FO.

"bad ware": Letter from Adams to Abigail, Jan. 6, 1794, FO.

"Murder, robbery": *Connecticut Courant*, Sept. 20, 1800.

atheist: Mason, John, *The Voice of Warning, to Christians*, Baker and Scribner, 1849, 560–561.

Jefferson was dead: *The Papers of Thomas Jefferson*, Vol. 32, *1 June 1800 to 16 February 1801*, Princeton UP, 2005, 42. The death in question was actually a slave of Jefferson's also named Thomas Jefferson.

"It is wellknown": *Richmond Recorder*, Sept. 1, 1802.

"dissembling patriot" "pretended 'man of the people'": Sheppard, *The Partisan Press*, 64.

"as despotic as": Malone, Dumas, *Jefferson and His Time: Jefferson the President, First Term, 1801–1805*, Little, Brown, 1970, 329.

"It is here": Burr, Aaron, Farewell speech to the Senate, Mar. 2, 1805.

"dastardly poltroon": Shaw, Peter, *The Character of John Adams*, University of North Carolina Press, 1976, 310.

"our wives": Boller, *Presidential Campaigns*, 12.

"contemptible hypocrite": Chernow, *Hamilton*, 634.

"confirmed infidel," "howling atheist": Vicchio, Stephen, *Jefferson's Religion*, Wipf and Stock, 2007, 6.

"brandy-soaked": Kuklick, Bruce, *A Political History of the USA: One Nation Under God*, Macmillan, 2009, 88.

"pernicious example": Chernow, *Hamilton*, 668.

"weak, wavering": Bernstein, R. B., *Thomas Jefferson: The Revolution of Ideas*, Oxford UP, 2004, 115.

"coward of Carter's mountain": Royster, Charles, *Light-Horse Harry Lee and the Legacy of the American Revolution*, Cambridge UP, 1982, 216.

James Madison (1751–1838; in Office 1809–1817)

"humble imitator," "cunning," "usurpations and tyranny": *Federal Republican*, Mar. 10, 12, 15, 1813, cited in Davis, David, "Presidents Madison and Monroe and the party press in transition, 1808–1824," in *Proceedings of the 1994 Conference of the American Journalism Historians Association, Part I*, Roanoke, Virginia, Oct. 6–8, 1994, ERIC, 311–335.

"wholly unfit": Hickey, Donald, *The War of 1812: A Forgotten Conflict*, University of Illinois Press, 1989, 104.

"Mrs. Madison is a fine," "withered apple John": Flynt and Eisenbach, *One Nation Under Sex*, 33.

"[weak], feeble": Bobb, David, *Humility: An Unlikely Biography of America's Greatest Virtue*, Thomas Nelson, 2013, 80.

"gloomy, stiff": "Theodorick Bland to Thomas Jefferson, 22 November 1780," FO.

"plain and rather mean-looking": Adams, Henry, and Earl Harbert, *History of the United States of America During the Administrations of James Madison*, Library of America, 1986, 87.

"political pimp": *Federal Republican*, Jan. 27, 1812.

"book politician": Bobb, *Humility*, 80.

"timid and indecisive": Cunningham, Noble, *The Jeffersonian Republicans in Power*, University of North Carolina Press, 1967, 232.

"mere puppet": Rutland, Robert, *James Madison: The Founding Father*, University of Missouri Press, 1997, 213.

"Whiffling Jemmy": Burstein and Isenberg, *Madison and Jefferson*, 500.

"Bonaparte": Sheppard, *The Partisan Press*, 67.

"little pigmy": Rutland, *James Madison*, 231.

James Monroe (1758–1831; in Office 1817–1825)

"in disgrace": Burstein and Isenberg, *Madison and Jefferson*, 561.

"The man himself . . . improper and incompetent . . . naturally dull," Burr, Aaron, *Memoirs of Aaron Burr*, Harper Bros., 1855, II: 433–434.

"liar": Ferling, *Jefferson and Hamilton*, 295. The minutes of the 1797 confrontation kept by Monroe's friend David Gelston recount that Hamilton said, "'Your representation is totally false (as nearly as I recollect the expression),' whereupon Monroe stood up and said 'Do you say I represented falsely, you are a Scoundrel.'" Good, Cassandra, "The near-duel between James Monroe and Alexander Hamilton," in *The Papers of James Monroe*, https: //academics.umw.edu/jamesmonroepapers/.

"weak & vain," "mere tool": Washington, "Comments on Monroe's A View of the Conduct of the Executive of the United States, March 1798," FO.

"disgraced": Letter to James Madison from James Monroe, 8 June 1798, FO.

"Nature has given him": Wirt, William, *Letter of the British Spy*, Fielding Lucas, 1811, 90.

"fawning parasite": *Alexandria Gazette*, Oct. 28, 1816.

"damned infernal": Boller, *Presidential Anecdotes*, 52.

"dull, sleepy," "hasn't got enough brains": Goodrich, *Recollections of a Lifetime; Or, Men and Things I Have Seen*, Arundel Press, 1856, 401–402.

"There is slowness": Nevins, Allan, ed., *The Diary of John Quincy Adams, 1794–1845*, Scribner, 1951, 191.

Chapter Three

John Quincy Adams (1767–1848; in Office 1825–1829)

"a man of reserved, cold, austere and forbidding manners": Nevins, *Diary of . . . Adams*, 217.

"Expired at Washington": Parsons, Lynn, *The Birth of Modern Politics: Andrew Jackson, John Quincy Adams, and the Election of 1828*, Oxford UP, 2011, 106.

"It is my duty": Benton, *Abridgment of the Debates of Congress*, 493.

"pimp of the coalition," "the panderer of an Autocrat": "The Pimp of the Coalition," in Benton, *Abridgment of the Debates of Congress*, 119.

"Old Man Eloquent": Remini, *John Quincy Adams*, 136 (the name alludes to Milton's description of Isocrates).

"King John II": Callahan, David, "John Quincy Adams and the elections of 1824 and 1828," in David Waldstreicher, ed., *A Companion to John Adams and John Quincy Adams*, Wiley, 2013, 321.

"Madman of Massachusetts": Falkner, Leonard, *The President Who Wouldn't Retire*, Coward-McCann, 1967, 154.

"apostate": Bigelow, John, "DeWitt Clinton as a politician," *Harper's Magazine* (Feb. 1875), 417.

"old lying scamp," "stricken down": Parsons, Lynn Hudson, "In which the political becomes the personal and vice versa: The last ten years of John Quincy Adams and Andrew Jackson," *Journal of the Early Republic* 23, no. 3 (2003): 421.

"Squintz": Nichols, Irby, *The European Pentarchy and the Congress of Verona, 1822*, Springer, 2012, 241.

"Coarse, dirty, and clownish": Ratcliffe, Donald, *The Politics of Long Division*, Ohio State UP, 2000, 225.

"perverse and mulish": Klein, *President James Buchanan*, 41.

Andrew Jackson (1767–1845; in Office 1829–1837)

"ungoverned temper, inflexible resolution, [and] vindictive spirit": Basch, Norma, "Marriage, morals, and politics in the election of 1828," in Kathleen Kennedy and Sharon Rena Ullman, eds., *Sexual Borderlands: Constructing an American Sexual Past*, Ohio State UP, 98.

"blood thirsty": Remini, *Andrew Jackson*, 128.

"General Jackson's mother": Remini, *Andrew Jackson*, 119–120.

"convicted adulteress," a "bigamist" and an "American Jezebel": Basch, "Marriage, morals, and politics in the election of 1828," 94.

"authority and power": "Senate reverses a presidential censure." https://www.senate.gov/artandhistory/history/minute/Senate_Reverses_A_Presidential_Censure.htm.

"Great Western Bluebeard," "Tennessee Slanderer," "man of the Pistol and Dirk," "fireside Hyena of character": Sparks, Edwin Erle, *The Men Who Made the Nation*, Macmillan, 1901, 289.

"monster," Onion, Rebecca, "The 'Coffin Handbill': Andrew Jackson's enemies used to circulate word of his 'bloody deeds,'" Slate.com, Mar. 5, 2014.

"ignorant, weak," "scarcely [more] fitted": Remini, *Andrew Jackson*, 309.

"man of violent": Tocqueville, Alexis de, *Democracy in America*, University of Chicago Press, 2000, 265.

"greater tyrant": Williams, Paul, *Jackson, Crockett and Houston on the American Frontier*, McFarland, 2016, 145.

"Bully": Collins, Gail, *Scorpion Tongues*, Harcourt Brace, 1999, 35.

"barbarian": Remini, *John Quincy Adams*, 78.

Martin Van Buren (1782–1862; in Office 1837–1841)

"Red Fox," "Little Magician": Widmer, *Martin Van Buren*, 4.

"laced up": Boller, *Presidential Campaigns*, 63.

"Golden Spoon Oration": Ogle, Charles, "The regal splendor of the president's palace," Speech given in US House of Representatives, Apr. 14–16, 1840.

"as dung," "secret, sly, selfish": Crockett, Davy, and Augustin Smith Clayton, *The Life of Martin Van Buren*, R. Wright, 1837, 13.

"bold, unscrupulous": Wilentz, Sean. *The Rise of American Democracy: Jefferson to Lincoln*. W. W. Norton & Company, 2006, 619.

"He is not": Koenig, Louis, "The rise of the little magician," *American Heritage* 13, no. 4 (June 1962).

"dandy," "struts and swaggers": Crockett and Clayton, *Life of Martin Van Buren*, 80.

"arch scoundrel," "prince of villains," "confirmed knave": Orth, Samuel, *Five American Politicians*, Burrows Brothers, 1906, 93.

"crawling reptile": Widmer, *Martin Van Buren*, 89.

"Martin Van Ruin": Nowlan, *The American Presidents, from Washington to Tyler*, 306.

"Van, Van, he's a used-up man": Widmer, *Martin Van Buren*, 138.

William Henry Harrison (1773–1841; in Office March 4, 1841–April 4, 1841)

"not without talents": Adams, *Memoirs of John Quincy Adams*, Vol. 7, Lippincott, 1877, 530.

"Granny Harrison," "petticoat general": Collins, *William Henry Harrison*, 103.

"rhyme but no reason": Boller, *Presidential Campaigns*, 72.

"General Mum," "a clodhopper": Collins, *William Henry Harrison*, 106, 75.

"bavard": Adams, *Memoirs*, Vol. 7, 530.

"greatest egotist," "a living mass of ruined matter": Collins, *William Henry Harrison*, 110, 107.

"political adventurer," "shallow mind": Adams, *Memoirs*, Vol. 7, 530.

"weak, vain old man," "a gossiping old lady": Sheppard, *The Partisan Press*, 109.

"present imbecile chief": Nowlan, *The American Presidents, from Washington to Tyler*, 360.

"superannuated and pitiable dotard": Jamieson, Kathleen Hall, *Packaging the Presidency: A History and Criticism of Presidential Campaign Advertising*, Oxford UP, 1996, 13.

John Tyler (1790–1862; in Office 1841–1845)
"Executive Ass," "unnatural relationship," "stick to writing": Black, *John Pendleton Kennedy*, 186.
"poor weeping willow": May, *John Tyler*, 5.
"his Accidency": Black, *John Pendleton Kennedy*, 186.
"Polonius president": Black, *John Pendleton Kennedy*, 193.
"imbecile in the Executive Chair": May, *John Tyler*, 5.
"political sectarian": Crapol, *John Tyler*, 57.
"traitor": Monroe, *Republican Vision*, 128.
"weak & conceited": Crapol, *John Tyler*, 104.
"destitute": Holt, *The Rise and Fall of the American Whig Party*, 137.
"renegade, John Tyler": Monroe, *Republican Vision*, 210.
"poor imbecile": Crapol, *John Tyler*, 102.
"mad, weak & a traitor," "irrational": Monroe, *Republican Vision*, 108, 104.
"deluded old jackass": May, *John Tyler*, 116.

James K. Polk (1795–1849; in Office 1845–1849)
"blighted burr," "dying gasp," "notorious Sabbath-breaker": Mayo, Louise, *President James K. Polk: The Dark-Horse President*, Nova, 2006, 53–54.
"bewildered," "half-insane," "encourage": Schroeder, John, *Mr. Polk's War: American Opposition and Dissent, 1846–1848*, University of Wisconsin Press, 1973, 63.
"coward, puppy": Byrnes, *James K. Polk*, 58.
"cancer," "petty tyrant," "had nothing": Byrnes, *James K. Polk*, 58, 144.
"coward, hiding": Greenberg, Amy, *A Wicked War: Polk, Clay, Lincoln, and the 1846 US Invasion of Mexico*, Random House, 2012, 251.
"The Hangman": Shenton, James, *Robert John Walker: A Politician from Jackson to Lincoln*, Columbia UP, 1961, 102.
"robber chief": Peterson, Merrill, *The Great Triumvirate: Webster, Clay, and Calhoun*, Oxford UP, 1989, 425.
"palpable knavery": Merry, Robert, *A Country of Vast Designs*, Simon & Schuster, 2010, 172.
"mendacious": Byrnes, *James K. Polk*, 144.

Zachary Taylor (1784–1850; in Office, 1849–July 9, 1850)
"illiterate frontier colonel": Boller, *Presidential Campaigns*, 85.

"Available candidate" cartoon, reprinted in *The Image of America in Caricature and Cartoon*, Amon Carter Museum of Western Art, 1975, 40.

"wholly incompetent": Remini, Robert, *Henry Clay: Statesman for the Union*, Norton, 1991, 711.

"military autocrat": Boller, *Presidential Campaigns*, 85.

"semi-stupefaction": Hamilton, *Zachary Taylor*, 216.

"dilatory, temporizing, timorous": *Washington Union*, Feb. 2, 1850.

"few men ever had": Nowlan, *The American Presidents, from Polk to Hayes*, 111.

"good old soul": Nowlan, *The American Presidents, from Polk to Hayes*, 111.

"dead and gone to hell": Hamilton, *Zachary Taylor*, 411.

Millard Fillmore (1800–1874; in Office 1850–1853)

"American Louis Philippe": *Millard Fillmore*, millercenter.org.

"man of hesitation": Holt, *The Rise and Fall of the American Whig Party*, 522.

"dallying": *New York Daily Herald*, Mar. 6, 1851.

"despotic pretensions": *Washington Union*, Sept. 6, 1850.

"second-hand president": Scarry, Robert, *Millard Fillmore*, McFarland, 2001, 192 (Scarry implies the story is apocryphal).

"wife-made": *Buffalo Courier*, July 4, 1850.

"lacks pluck": Nowlan, *The American Presidents, from Polk to Hayes*, 161.

"cowardly": *New York Evening Post*, Sept. 9, 1850.

"timid": Washington *Daily Republic*, May 7, 1851.

"small neighborhood candidate": Risley, Ford, *Abolition and the Press: The Moral Struggle Against Slavery*, Northwestern UP, 2008, 142.

"loathe your dough-face": Miles, William, *Songs, Odes, Glees, and Ballads: A Bibliography of American Presidential Campaign Songsters*, Greenwood, 1990, xxxv.

Franklin Pierce (1804–1869; in Office 1853–1857)

"well-fought bottle": Gara, Larry, *The Presidency of Franklin Pierce*, UP of Kansas, 1991, 38.

"political Jonah": Holt, *Franklin Pierce*, 102.

"Fainting Frank": Nowlan, *The American Presidents, from Polk to Hayes*, 104.

"dupe": Holt, *Franklin Pierce*, 104.

"New Hampshire, Democratic, doughface": Nowlan, *The American Presidents, from Polk to Hayes*, 211.

"arch traitor": Moers, Ellen, *Harriet Beecher Stowe and American Literature*, Stowe-Day Foundation, 1978, 29.

"but of one excuse": Nowlan, *The American Presidents, from Polk to Hayes*, 221.

"vain, slow, and pliant": Nowlan, *The American Presidents, from Polk to Hayes*, 212.

"wholly without moral courage": *New York Herald*, Feb. 21, 1856.

"black-hearted copperhead": DeRose, Chris, *The Presidents' War: Six American Presidents and the Civil War That Divided the Nation*, Rowman & Littlefield, 2014, 272.

James Buchanan (1791–1868; in Office 1857–1861)

"Aunt Fancy," "Miss Nancy," "Siamese twins," "Buchanan's wife": Baker, *James Buchanan*, 25; Flynt and Eisenbach, *One Nation*, 50.

"doughface," "coward": Baker, *James Buchanan*, 56.

"chief of the traitors": *Richmond Enquirer*, Sept. 15, 1857.

"most amazing": "Review of current literature," *Christian Examiner* 80 (1866): 405–406.

"inept busybody": Buell, Augustus, *History of Andrew Jackson*, Vol. 2, Scribner's, 1904, 404.

"Ten Cent Jimmy": Klein, *President James Buchanan*, 134.

"bloated mass": Han, *Hatred*, 102.

"old dotard": Birkner, Michael, *James Buchanan and the Political Crisis of the 1850s*, Susquehanna UP, 1996, 71.

"granny executive": Grant, Ulysses, *Personal Memoirs of U. S. Grant*, Vol. 1, Charles L. Webster, 1885, 215.

"cowardly old imbecile": Han, *Hatred*, 105.

"Judas": Klein, *President James Buchanan*, 12; Heritage Slater Political Memorabilia and Americana Auction Catalog #619, Ivy Press, 2005, 43.

"old public functionary": Buchanan, James, Third Annual Message to Congress on the State of the Union, Dec. 19, 1859.

"pusillanimous dotard": *California Argus*, Feb. 19, 1861.

Chapter Four

Abraham Lincoln (1809–1865; in Office 1861–April 15, 1865)

"charging," "public office," "slang-whanging": *North American Review*, June 1912, 738.

"vulgar village politician," "third-rate Western lawyer," "unmitigated trash": Tagg, *The Unpopular Mr. Lincoln*, 73.

"hatchet-faced," "abused the privilege": Fetters, Ashley, "Great emancipator or creepy slob? Historic portrayals of Abraham Lincoln," *Atlantic*, Nov. 8, 2012.

"well-meaning baboon," "original gorilla." Tagg, *The Unpopular Mr. Lincoln*, 131.

"horrid looking": *Charleston Mercury*, June 9, 1860.

"wishy-washy": Tagg, *The Unpopular Mr. Lincoln*, 110.

"illiterate," "inhuman," "wicked," "irreligious," "without brains," "coarse": Burlingame, Michael, *Lincoln and the Civil War*, Southern Illinois UP, 2011, 104.

"barbarian," "Dishonest Abe," "timid vacillating & inefficient," "imbecile President": Burlingame, Michael, *Abraham Lincoln: A Life*, Johns Hopkins UP, 2013, 285, 685, 215, 417.

"Presidential pigmy," "half-witted Usurper," "brainless tyrant": Tagg, *The Unpopular Mr. Lincoln*, 101, 345.

Andrew Johnson (1808–1875; in Office 1865–1869)

"insolent drunken brute": Tebbel and Watts, *The Press and the Presidency*, 209.

"Andy the sot": Whitcomb and Whitcomb, *Real Life at the White House*, 149.

"no drunk": Dunn, Charles, *The Scarlet Thread of Scandal: Morality and the American Presidency*, Rowman and Littlefield, 2001, 60.

"intemperate," "Andrew Johnson": *Harper's Weekly*, Sept. 15, 1866.

"Judas Johnson," "Yes, why not," "Drunken Tailor": Tebbel and Watts, *The Press and the Presidency*, 211.

"vindictive and perverse": Polk, *Diary*, 226.

"insolent, clownish creature": Tebbel and Watts, *The Press and the Presidency*, 206, 209.

"Whatever Andrew Johnson may be": Gordon-Reed, Annette, *Andrew Johnson*, Holt, 2011, 2.

"If Andy Johnson was a snake": Nowlan, *The American Presidents, from Polk to Hayes*, 437.

"bloody-minded tailor": Chesnut, Mary, *A Diary from Dixie*, D. Appleton, 1906, 398.

"renegade and traitor": Fleming, Walter, *Civil War and Reconstruction in Alabama*, Columbia UP, 1905, 546.

"infernal liar": Smith, *Grant*, 454.

"alien enemy": Whitcomb and Whitcomb, *Real Life at the White House*, 150.

"great apostate," "faithless demagogue," "great accidental," "great pardoner": Laracey, Mel, *Presidents and the People*, Texas A&M UP, 2002, 115.

"demagogue and autocrat": Whipple, E. P., "The Johnson party," *Atlantic*, Sept. 1866.

"impersonation": Nowlan, *The American Presidents, from Polk to Hayes*, 424.

Ulysses S. Grant (1822–1885; in Office 1869–1877)

"mendacious, cunning, and treacherous": Johnson, Andrew, *The Papers of Andrew Johnson: May 1869–July 1875*, University of Tennessee Press, 1967, 40–41.

"baby politician": Adams, Henry, *The Education of Henry Adams: An Autobiography*, Houghton Mifflin, 1918, 262.

Harper's cartoon: *Harper's Weekly*, Feb. 15, 1868, reprinted in Waugh, John, *U. S. Grant: American Hero, American Myth*, University of North Carolina Press, 2009, 105. The humor magazine *Puck* also portrayed Grant as a baby on its April 7, 1880, cover.

"fire of personal abuse": Chernow, *Grant*, 810.

"Mistakes have been made": Grant, Ulysses, Eighth Annual Message, Dec. 5, 1876.

"Useless Grant," "the Butcher": Chernow, *Grant*, 3, 408.

"scientific Goth": Suster, Gerald, *Generals: The Best and Worst Military Commanders*, Robson Books, 1997, 176.

"surly": Brighton, Raymond, *Rambles About Portsmouth*, Portsmouth Marine Society, Peter Randall Publisher, 1993.

"Grant the Drunkard": *Akron Times*, Aug. 24, 1872.

"uniquely stupid": Chernow, *Grant*, 679–680.

"political ignoramus": Chernow, *Grant*, 599.

"dangerous man": Welles, Gideon, *Diary of Gideon Welles*, Vol. 3, Houghton Mifflin, 1911, 245.

"ignorant soldier": *Nation*, Mar. 9, 1876.

"not an idea": Hesseltine, William, *Ulysses S. Grant*, Simon Publications, 2001, 342.

"great presidential quarreler," "utterly indefensible": Sumner, Charles, *Republicanism vs. Grantism*, Lee and Shepard, 1872, 5.

"He had done more": Garfield, James A., *The Diary of James A. Garfield: 1875–1877*, Michigan State UP, 1967, 244.

Rutherford B. Hayes (1822–1893; in Office 1877–1881)

"greatest failure": Hoogenboom, Ari, *Rutherford B. Hayes: Warrior and President*, UP of Kansas, 1995, 353.

"His Fraudulency," "the Pretender": Spragens, *Popular Images*, 105.

"usurper" with "a disturbed mind," "useless to attempt": Morgan, Howard, *From Hayes to McKinley*, Syracuse UP, 1969, 34–35.

"third rate nonentity," "not a ray": Spragens, *Popular Images*, 105.

"illegitimate president": Congressional Quarterly, *American Political Leaders 1789–2009*, CQ Press, 2009, 52.

"bogus, fraudulent, so called President": Spragens, *Popular Images*, 105.

"cheat": Morris, Roy, *Fraud of the Century*, Simon & Schuster, 2003, 241.

"weak and imbecile": *Millheim (PA) Journal*, Mar. 8, 1977.

"Granny Hayes": Barker, Paula, "Chester A. Arthur," in Brinkley and Dyer, eds., *The American Presidency*, 237.

"Queen Victoria in breeches": Martin, Ralph, *Jennie*, New American Library, 1969, 122.

"worse than a usurper": *Atlanta Constitution*, Apr. 30, 1879.

"amiable imbecile": *Lexington Intelligencer*, June 11, 1881.

"one of the most unmitigated": *Chicago Tribune*, Jan. 9, 1882.

Garfield (1831–1881, in office March 4, 1881-Sept. 19, 1881)

"chief of the conspirators," "$325": Hutchins, *The 1880 Democratic Campaign Handbook*, 79, 52.

"base fellow": Peskin, *Garfield*, 215.

"perfidy without parallel": Peskin, *Garfield*, 561.

"ready champion": Hutchins, *The 1880 Democratic Campaign Handbook*, 251.

"angleworm": Clancy, Herbert J., *The Presidential Election of 1880*, Loyola UP, 1958, 116.

"backbone of an angleworm": Peskin, *Garfield*, 561.

"clever trickster": *Concord (NH) People and Patriot*, June 9, 1880.

"perjurer": Hutchins, *The 1880 Democratic Campaign Handbook*, 79.

"character is as dubious": *St. Louis Post-Dispatch*, June 8, 1880.

"Janus-faced": Hutchins, *The 1880 Democratic Campaign Handbook*, 258.

"not only a liar": *Boston Globe*, Oct. 28, 1880.

"big, confused Newfoundland dog": Smith, Theodore, *The Life and Letters of James Abram Garfield: 1877–1882*, Archon Books, 1968, 1142.

"president-czar": Leech, Margaret, and Harry Brown, *The Garfield Orbit*, Harper & Row, 1977, 241.

"not been square": "The secret history of the Garfield-Conkling tragedy," *The Literary Digest* 15, no. 7 (1897): 205.

Chester A. Arthur (1829–1886; in Office 1881–1885)

"bland," "stalking horse": Greenberger, Scott, *The Unexpected President: The Life and Times of Chester A. Arthur*, Da Capo Press, 2017, 85.

"miserable farce": Karabell, Zachary, *Chester Alan Arthur*, Macmillan, 2004, 47.

"about the last man": Boller, *Presidential Anecdotes*, 173.

"Conkling's man Friday": *St. Louis Post-Dispatch*, June 9, 1880.

"coward and an ingrate": *New York Times*, July 1, 1882.

"better fitted to be a scullion": Falzone, Vincent, *Terence V. Powderly, Middle Class Reformer*, UP of America, 1978, 82.

"stalled ox": Reeves, Thomas, *Gentleman Boss: The Life of Chester Alan Arthur*, Knopf, 1975, 304.

not an American: Curran, John, "Chester Arthur rumor still lingers in Vermont," *Boston Globe*, Aug. 17, 2009.

"mental equipment": *New York Tribune*, Nov. 19, 1886.

"flathead": Roberts, Robert, Scott Hammond, and Valerie Sulfaro, *Presidential Campaigns, Slogans, Issues, and Platforms: The Complete Encyclopedia*, Vol. 1, ABC-CLIO, 2012, 799.

Grover Cleveland (1837–1908; in Office 1885–1889, 1893–1897)

"rake," "libertine," "father of a bastard," "gross," "moral leper," "stained": Boller, *Presidential Campaigns*, 149.

"Stuffed Prophet," *Sun*, Aug. 11, 1890.

"newspaper lying": Brodsky, Alyn, *Grover Cleveland: A Study in Character*, Macmillan, 2000, 125.

"Republican virus," "not the remotest notion": Welch, *The Presidencies of Grover Cleveland*, 209.

"coarse debauchee": Boller, *Presidential Campaigns*, 149.

"plodding mind": Nevins, Allan, *Grover Cleveland: A Study in Courage*, Dodd Mead, 1932, 148.

"besotted tyrant": Olasky, Marvin, *The American Leadership Tradition: The Inevitable Impact of a Leader's Faith on a Nation's Destiny*, Crossway, 2000, 164.

"damned traitor": *Democrat and Chronicle* (Rochester, NY), May 8, 1896.

"puppet": *Kearney (NE) Daily Hub*, Sept. 8, 1892.

"To laud Clevelandism": Welch, *The Presidencies of Grover Cleveland*, 209.

"bunko steerer": *Inter Ocean* (Chicago), Aug. 6, 1903.

"Fat Incubus": *New York Sun*, July 25, 1891.

"agent": Strouse, Jean, *Morgan: American Financier*, Random House, 1999, 349.

"fat old bull": *Fitchburg Sentinel*, May 22, 1893.

Benjamin Harrison (1833–1901; in Office 1889–1893)

"human iceberg": Spetter, Allan, *Benjamin Harrison: Life Before the Presidency*, millercenter.org.

"could no longer endure," "victim": *Freeborn County (MN) Standard*, June 15, 1892.

"Little Ben": Wallace, Lew, *Life of Gen. Ben Harrison*, Hubbard Bros., 1888, 198.

"Grandfather's Hat": Miller, Nathan, *Star-Spangled Men: America's Ten Worst Presidents*, Simon & Schuster, 1999, 69.

"stinking little aristocrat": Sievers, Harry Joseph, *Benjamin Harrison: Hoosier Statesman*, Regnery, 1952, 56.

"Kid Glove Harrison": Moore, Anne Chieko, and Hester Anne Hale, *Benjamin Harrison: Centennial President*, Nova Publishers, 2006, 54.

"everlasting friend": *Terre Haute Weekly Gazette*, Nov. 1, 1888.

"refrigerator": Orren, Karen, "Benjamin Harrison," in Brinkley and Davis Dyer, eds., *The American Presidency*, 250.

"narrow, unresponsive," "like talking to a hitching post": Boller, *Presidential Anecdotes*, 185.

"cold-blooded": *Vicksburg Evening Post*, Mar. 3, 1891.

"grouchy": Dozer, Donald, "Harrison and the presidential campaign of 1892," *American Historical Review* 54, no. 1 (1948): 49–77.

"glacial": Platt, Thomas Collier, *The Autobiography of Thomas Collier Platt*, B. W. Dodge, 1910, 252.

"obstinate": Calhoun, Charles, *Benjamin Harrison,* Macmillan, 2005, 132.

"cold-blooded, narrow-minded": Morris, Edmund, *The Rise of Theodore Roosevelt*, Random House, 2010, 436.

"little gray man," "cold": Beschloss, Michael, *American Heritage Illustrated History of the Presidents*, Crown, 2000, 299.

William McKinley (1843–1901; in Office 1897–September 14, 1901)

"leaders": Jones, Stanley, *The Presidential Election of 1896*, University of Wisconsin Press, 1964, 143.

"weak and a bidder": Gould, Lewis, "William McKinley: Foreign affairs," The Miller Center, millercenter.org.

"white-livered cur": Boller, *Presidential Anecdotes*, 190.

"no more backbone": Hamilton, Robert, "McKinley's backbone," *Presidential Studies Quarterly* 36, no. 3 (2006): 482–492.

"Mr. Face-both-ways": Wall, Joseph, *Andrew Carnegie*, Oxford UP, 1970, 696.

"man of jelly": Gould, Lewis, *The Presidency of William McKinley*, UP of Kansas, 1980, 157.

"destined for a statue": White, William Allen, and Sally Foreman Griffith, *The Autobiography of William Allen White*, Macmillan, 1946, 292.

"most hated creature": Ford, Edwin, and Edwin Emery, *Highlights in the History of the American Press*, University of Minnesota Press, 1954, 283.

"dangerous set": *The United States Army and Navy Journal and Gazette of the Regular and Volunteer Forces*, Sept. 28, 1901.

"sad jellyfish": Thomas, Evan, *The War Lovers: Roosevelt, Lodge, Hearst, and the Rush to Empire, 1898*, Little Brown, 2010, 137.

"piece of affable": Scharnhorst, *Julian Hawthorne*, 146.

"Ohio twaddler": *Brooklyn Daily Eagle*, Sept. 18, 1901.

"ear so close": Kinzer, *The True Flag*, 83.

"president of the money kings": Goldman, Emma, and Candace Falk, *Emma Goldman: A Documentary History of the American Years*, Vol. 1, University of California Press, 2008, 79.

"echo": Lindsay, Vachel, "Bryan, Bryan, Bryan, Bryan," in *Collected Poems*, Macmillan, 1941, 97–98.

"enemy of the good people": *NYT*, Oct. 30, 1901.

Chapter Five

Theodore Roosevelt (1858–1919; in Office 1901–1909)

"damned cowboy": Safire, William, *Safire's Political Dictionary*, Oxford UP, 2008, 154.

"only one life": Manners, William, *TR and Will: A Friendship That Split the Republican Party*, Harcourt, Brace & World, 1969, 39.

"dangerous and ominous," "little emasculated": Morris, Edmund, "Bookend: Charge!," *NYT Book Review*, Nov. 7, 1999.

"string of infamous libels," "decision is so sweeping": Tebbel and Watts, *The Press and the Presidency*, 345–348.

"Jane-Dandy": McCullogh, David, *Mornings on Horseback*, Simon & Schuster, 2007, 256.

"Oscar Wilde," "exquisite Mr. Roosevelt," "chief of the dudes": Morris, Edmund, *The Rise of Theodore Roosevelt*, Random House, 2010, 178; and Kimmel, Michael, *The Politics of Manhood*, Temple UP, 1995, 134.

"monstrous embodiment": Morris, "Bookend: Charge!"

"utterly without conscience": Pietrusza, David, *1920: The Year of the Six Presidents*, Carroll & Graf, 2006, 75.

"pirate," "Roosevelt denounced in House": *Santa Cruz Evening News*, July 24, 1912.

"drunk": "No liquor taint on the breath of the Colonel," *San Francisco Chronicle*, May 29, 1913.

"servile functionary": Chace, *1912*, 223.

"bellhop": Taylor, Jeff, *Politics on a Human Scale: The American Tradition of Decentralism*, Lexington Books, 2013, 148.

"clearly insane," "most formidable disaster": Kinzer, *The True Flag*, 13.

"demagogue and a flatterer," "dangerous egotist": Chace, *1912*, 112.

"freak": Coletta, *The Presidency of William Howard Taft*, 242.

"honeyfuggler": Gould, Lewis, "The 1912 Republican Convention," *Smithsonian Magazine*, Aug. 2007.

"thimblerigger": *Official Report of the Proceedings of the Fifteenth Republican National Convention Held in Chicago*, The Tenny Press, 1912, 437.

"charlatan," "mountebank," "quite typical member": Mencken, H. L., *Mencken Chrestomathy*, Knopf, 2012, 245, 242.

William Howard Taft (1857–1930; in Office 1909–1913)

"Smiling Bill": *WaPo*, June 28, 1908.

"Big Chief": Benson, Michael, *William H. Taft*, Lerner, 2005, 99.

"blunderer": *Modern Light* (Kansas), July 9, 1908.

"fathead," "puzzlewit," "flubdub": Anderson, Judith, "William Howard Taft," in Philip Weeks, ed., *Buckeye Presidents: Ohioans in the White House*, Kent State UP, 2003, 231.

"golf pig": Scharnhorst, *Julian Hawthorne*, 197.

"Mr. Malaprop": Coletta, *The Presidency of William Howard Taft*, 55.

"Van Buren": *Atlantic*, Feb. 1912.

"big, fat, and lazy": *Wichita Daily Eagle*, Jan. 27, 1911.

"means well feebly," "easy-going fat man": *Macon Times-Democrat*, Oct. 24, 1912.

"blundering politician": Anderson, "William Howard Taft," 212.

Woodrow Wilson (1856–1924; in Office 1913–1921)

"dictator," "coward," "rumors": Tebbel and Watts, *The Press and the Presidency*, 369.

"dishonorable": Fleming, Thomas, *The Illusion of Victory*, Basic Books, 2003, 3.

"liar and an ingrate": *NYT*, July 27, 1911.

"most of the prejudices," "Wilson and the Negro": *New York Age*, July 11, 1912.

"devil," "satanic": "Wilson the Devil, Bryan Rattlesnake," *St. Louis Star and Times*, July 3, 1912.

"usurper": "Wilson dictator declares Sherman," *Asbury Park Press*, Mar. 3, 1919.

"human icicle": *Voice of San Diego*, Sept. 18, 2009.

"bearded icicle": Ross, William G., *The Chief Justiceship of Charles Evans Hughes, 1930–1941*, University of South Carolina Press, 2007, 2.

"prime jackass," "coward," "skin him alive": Lasner, Lynn, "The passions of Woodrow Wilson," *Humanities* 22, no. 6 (2001); and Renehan, Edward, Jr., *The Lion's Pride*, Oxford UP, 1999, 129.

"effeminate": "To call Mr. Wilson a weathercock": *Boston Post*, Aug. 20, 1916.

"idiotic babbling": Mencken, H. L., *Prejudices: A Selection*, Johns Hopkins UP, 115.

"strutting pedagogue," "unctuous charlatan": Scharnhorst, *Julian Hawthorne*, 197.

"less virile": Berg, A. Scott, *Wilson*, Penguin, 2013, 294.

"yellow": Tuchman, Barbara, *The Zimmermann Telegram*, Random House, 1985, 147.

"elocutionist," "neither a gentleman": Sullivan, Mark, *Our Times, 1900–1925: Over Here, 1914–1918*, Vol. 5, Scribner, 1972, 204.

"incompetent": Rascoe, Burton, "Wilson duped by 'big 3' says noted Briton," *Chicago Tribune*, Feb. 14, 1920.

Warren G. Harding (1865–1923; in Office 1921–August 2, 1923)

"not heroics, but healing": Harding, Warren G., "National ideals and policies," *Protectionist* (May 1920): 71–81. Available online via The Miller Center.

"bloviating": Chace, *1912*, 272.

"army of pompous phrases": Goldman, Eric, "A sort of rehabilitation of Warren G. Harding," *NYT Magazine*, Mar. 26, 1972.

"man of limited talents," "I am not fit": Leuchtenburg, *The American President*, 118.

"respectable Ohio politician": *NYT*, June 13, 1920.

"spineless": Miller, Linda Karen, *Populist Nationalism: Republican Insurgency and American Foreign Policy*, Greenwood, 1999, 93.

"not a white man": *NYT*, Oct. 30, 1920.

"slob": Longworth, *Crowded Hours*, 325.

"he-harlot": Ferrell, Robert, *Presidential Leadership: From Woodrow Wilson to Harry S. Truman*, University of Missouri Press, 2006, 39.

"cheese-paring": Russell, Francis, "The four mysteries of Warren Harding," *American Heritage*, April 1963.

"human smudge": Goldman, "A sort of rehabilitation of Warren G. Harding."

"The Vegetable": Tebbel and Watts, *The Press and the Presidency*, 398.

"Bungalow-minded": Poore, Patricia, "The bungalow and why we love it so," *Old House Journal* (May 1985).

"disturbingly dull mind": Stevens, Rosemary, *A Time of Scandal: Charles R. Forbes, Warren G. Harding, and the Making of the Veterans Bureau*, Johns Hopkins UP, 2016, 28.

"aging cockroach": Rodgers, Marion Elizabeth, *Mencken: The American Iconoclast*, Oxford UP, 2007, 222.

"setting aside a college professor": Mencken, *On Politics*, 42.

"only man, woman or child": Cummings, Edward Estlin, "XXVII," in *Complete Poems*, Vol. 1, MacGibbon & Kee, 1968, 336.

Calvin Coolidge (1872–1933; in Office 1923–1929)

"Nobody has ever": Lippmann, Walter, *Man of Destiny*, Transaction Publishers, 2003, 13.

"midget statesman," "man in public life": Tebbel and Watts, *The Press and the Presidency*, 410.

"Isn't it past": Whitcomb and Whitcomb, *Real Life at the White House*, 275.

"little fellow": Purcell, L. Edward, *Vice Presidents: A Biographical Dictionary*, Facts on File, 2010, 284.

"cheap veep": Whitcomb and Whitcomb, *Real Life at the White House*, 274.

"smallest caliber": Sobel, Robert, *Coolidge: An American Enigma*, Regnery, 1998, 246.

"icy hand," "mentality": *Literary Digest*, Aug. 18, 1923, 8.

"attitude": White, William Allen, *A Puritan in Babylon*, Macmillan, 1938, 371.

"runty aloof": Tebbel and Watts, *The Press and the Presidency*, 410.

"New England backwoodsman": Churchill, Randolph, and Martin Gilbert, *Winston S. Churchill*, Houghton Mifflin, 1981, 1380.

"stubborn," "dreadful": Mencken, *On Politics*, 82, 118.

"weaned on a pickle": Longworth, *Crowded Hours*, 337.

"continually worn": Weatherson, Michael, and Hal Bochin, *Hiram Johnson: Political Revivalist*, UP of America, 1995, 219.

Herbert Hoover (1874–1964; in Office 1929–1933)

"smartest gink," "Wonder Boy": Leuchtenburg, *The American President*, 121.

"unsolicited advice": Hawley, Ellis, *Herbert Hoover as Secretary of Commerce*, University of Iowa Press, 1981, 34, 37.

"Al-coholic Smith": Hamilton, David, *Herbert Hoover: Campaigns and Elections*, millercenter.org.

"ceaseless torrent," "President cannot": Hoover, Herbert, *The Great Depression, 1929–1941*, Macmillan, 1952, 220.

"Hoover cart" and "one engineer": *Public Papers of the Presidents: Harry S. Truman*, US Government Printing Office, 1964 [1948], 822–827, 882–886.

"nothing but politics": Trohan, Walter, *Political Animals*, Doubleday, 1975, 206.

"son-of-a-bitch": Burner, David, *Herbert Hoover: The Public Life*, Knopf, 1979, 82.

"fascist": New York *Daily News*, Feb. 11, 1929.

"jellyfish": *Baltimore Sun*, July 7, 1932; Allen, Frederick Lewis, *Since Yesterday*, Harper, 1939, 40; and the *El Paso Evening Post*, Oct. 15, 1928.

"irresolute": Lippmann, Walter, "The peculiar weakness of Mr. Hoover," *Harper's*, June 1930.

"spineless cactus": *Miami (OK) Daily News-Record*, Sept. 10, 1931.

"inept": *Messenger-Inquirer* (Kentucky), Oct. 16, 1932.

"fatter, softer Coolidge": Cowing, Cedric, "H. L. Mencken: The case of the 'curdled' progressive," *Ethics* 69, no. 4 (959): 255–267.

"shiny, shallow," "sort of man": Mencken, *On Politics*, 256, 268.

"recent acquisition": Fausold, Martin, *The Presidency of Herbert C. Hoover*, UP of Kansas, 1985, 13.

"big liar": *Akron Beacon Journal*, Sept. 8, 1932.

"tyrant": *Stevens Point (WI) Journal*, Aug. 15, 1932.

"President Reject": Tebbel and Watts, *The Press and the Presidency*, 433.

Franklin D. Roosevelt (1882–1945; in Office 1933–April 12, 1945)

"tired old men": Jordan, David, *FDR, Dewey, and the Election of 1944*, Indiana UP, 2011, 164.

"with Marx and Lenin": Slayton, Robert, *Empire Statesman: The Rise and Redemption of Al Smith*, Free Press, 2001, 388.

"great betrayer," "scab President": Leuchtenburg, *The FDR Years*, 121.

"consuming personal hatred": Childs, Marquis, *They Hate Roosevelt*, Harper & Brothers, 1936, 1.

"proud to have earned": Roosevelt, Franklin D., Jan. 3, 1936, Message to Congress.

"kind of amiable": Parrish, Michael, *Anxious Decades: America in Prosperity and Depression, 1920–1941*, Norton, 1994, 285.

"Moosejaw," "momma's boy": Laskow, Sarah, "The true origins of the phrase 'bleeding-heart liberal,'" Atlas Obscura.com, Feb. 15, 2017.

"chameleon on plaid": Leuchtenburg, *The FDR Years*, 2.

"gibbering idiot": Whitcomb and Whitcomb, *Real Life at the White House*, 298.

"ignorant": Whyte, Kenneth, *Hoover: An Extraordinary Life in Extraordinary Times*, Knopf, 2017, 517.

"liar and a fake": Black, Conrad, *Franklin Delano Roosevelt: Champion of Freedom*, PublicAffairs, 2012, 358.

"Communist [in] the chair": Leuchtenburg, *The FDR Years*, 121.

"traitor to his class": Daniels, Roger, *Franklin D. Roosevelt: Road to the New Deal, 1882–1939*, University of Illinois Press, 2015, 209.

SOURCES AND BIBLIOGRAPHY

"Kerensky": Chafe, William Henry, *The Achievement of American Liberalism: The New Deal and Its Legacies*, Columbia UP, 2003, 102.

"Wall Street tool": Schlesinger, Arthur M., *The Politics of Upheaval: 1935–1936, the Age of Roosevelt*, Vol. III, Houghton Mifflin, 2004, 190.

"crazy, conceited megalomaniac": Rosentreter, Roger, *Michigan: A History of Explorers, Entrepreneurs, and Everyday People*, University of Michigan Press, 2013, 300.

"prize honeyfuggler": Quinion, Michael, *World Wide Words*, Oct. 9, 2004; *Syracuse Herald*, Jan. 14, 1934, 61.

"ninety per cent Eleanor": Bannister, Robert, *Sociology and Scientism: The American Quest for Objectivity, 1880–1940*, University of North Carolina Press, 2014, 202; Keyes, Ralph, *The Quote Verifier: Who Said What, Where, and When*, St. Martin's, 2006, 133; and *NYT*, Feb. 20, 1980.

"Quack," "political racket," "bogus miracles," "became convinced": Rogers, Marion, *Mencken: The American Iconoclast*, Oxford UP, 2007, 430.

"utter incompetent": Cushman, Clare, ed., *The Supreme Court Justices: Illustrated Biographies, 1789–2012*, CQ Press, 2012, 297.

"second-class intellect": Boller, *Not So!*, 102.

"Frank D. Rosenfeld," "Jew Deal": Blamires, Cyprian, and Paul Jackson, eds., *World Fascism: A Historical Encyclopedia*, Vol. 1, ABC-CLIO, 2006, 270.

"lawless dictator": Dunn, Susan, *1940: FDR, Willkie, Lindbergh, Hitler: The Election Amid the Storm*, Yale UP, 2013, 184.

"dictator": Thurman, Judith, "A libertarian house on the prairie," *New Yorker*, Aug. 16, 2012.

"crippled son-of-a-bitch": Miller, *Plain Speaking*, 186.

"rainy-day plutocrat," "his buck-toothed bride": *Nation* 189 (1959): 193.

Chapter Six

Harry S. Truman (1884–1972; in Office 1945–1953)

"I refer to McCarthy": Herman, Arthur, *Joseph McCarthy: Reexamining the Life and Legacy of America's Most Hated Senator*, Free Press, 1999, 146.

"Pendergast's bellhop": McCullough, *Truman*, 248.

"vulgar little Babbitt": Black, Conrad, *Backward Glances: People and Events from Inside and Out*, Signal, 2016, 507.

"political accident," "invariably awkward": *Time*, Mar. 15, 1948.

"son-of-a-bitch": McCullough, *Truman*, 847.

"monster," "butcher": Kaplan, Carla, ed., *Zora Neale Hurston: A Life in Letters*, Doubleday, 2007, 546.

"nincompoop": *Chicago Daily Tribune*, June 11, 1948.

"gutter fighter": Pearlman, Michael, *Truman and MacArthur*, IU Press, 2008, 13.

"thin-lipped hater," "phony": Pegler, Westbrook, syndicated column (*Tampa Tribune*), Jan. 24, 1949.

"rat": Truman, Harry S., *Off the Record: The Private Papers of Harry S. Truman*, University of Missouri Press, 1997, 113.

"guttersnipe": McCullough, *Truman*, 829.

"traitor": Ferrell, Robert, *Harry S. Truman: A Life*, University of Missouri Press, 1996, 391.

"I don't think": Miller, *Plain Speaking*, 135.

Dwight D. Eisenhower (1890–1969; in Office 1953–1961)

"Nothing will be so effective": "Eisenhower and McCarthy: How the president toppled a reckless senator," *Prologue* (Washington, DC) 47, no. 3 (2015): 16–24.

"clerk": Terzian, Philip, *Architects of Power*, Encounter Books, 2010, 62.

"studied theatrics": Peretti, Burton, *The Leading Man: Hollywood and the Presidential Image*, Rutgers UP, 2012, 100.

"Dopey Dwight," "stinking hypocrite," "playboy," "fathead": Cash, *Who the Hell Is William Loeb?*, xvi.

"good-looking mortician," "a pig in a poke": Ingalls, David, "A haymaker goes wild," *LIFE*, Jan. 28, 1952.

"hero worship," "glamour," "sex appeal": Blake, David, *Liking Ike: Eisenhower, Advertising, and the Rise of Celebrity*, Oxford UP, 2016, 67.

"stooge for Wall Street," "coward": Algeo, Matthew, *Harry Truman's Excellent Adventure*, Chicago Review Press, 2009.

"dumb son-of-a-bitch": Aurthur, Robert, "The wit and sass of Harry Truman," *Esquire* 76 (August 1971): 62–67, 115–118.

"puppet," "dangling and dancing": *Statesman Journal* (Oregon), Oct. 19, 1952.

"yellow son-of-a-bitch": Herken, Gregg, *The Georgetown Set: Friends and Rivals in Cold War*, Knopf, 2014, 193.

"part-time president," "indifferent": *Courier-Journal* (Louisville, Kentucky), Oct. 28, 1956.

"dime-store New Dealer": Skipper John, *The 1964 Republican Convention: Barry Goldwater and the Beginning of the Modern Conservative Movement*, McFarland, 2016, 29.

"Communist agent": Whitfield, Stephen, *The Culture of the Cold War*, Johns Hopkins UP, 1996, 42.

"old asshole," "pretty boy," "young whippersnapper," "Little Boy Blue": Reeves, Richard, *President Kennedy: Profile of Power*, Simon & Schuster, 1994, 22.

"devious": Nixon, Richard, *Six Crises*, Doubleday, 1962, 161.

"worst President," "nice old gentleman," "dead whale," "lowest form of animal life": Mieczkowski, Yanek, *Eisenhower's Sputnik Moment*, Cornell UP, 2013, 244.

John F. Kennedy (1917–1963; in Office 1961–November 22, 1963)

"another Truman": Gardner, *Campaign Comedy*, 287.

"goddamn Mick": Porter, Darwin, and Danforth Prince, *Jacqueline Kennedy Onassis*, Blood Moon Productions, Limited, 2014, 11.

"little scrawny fellow": Dallek, Robert, *An Unfinished Life: John F. Kennedy, 1917-1963*, Little Brown, 2003, 261.

"Papa's pet," "acting like": Lasky, Victor, *JFK: The Man and the Myth*, Macmillan, 1963, 246, 343.

"spoiled": Eisenhower, David, *Going Home to Glory*, Simon & Schuster, 2013, 17.

"enviably attractive nephew": Leuchtenburg, *The American President*, 375.

"young genius," "wizard": Shaw, John, *Rising Star, Setting Sun*, Pegasus Books, 2018, 74.

"not a man's man": Caro, Robert, *The Passage of Power*, Knopf, 1982, 33.

"barefaced liar": Gardner, *Campaign Comedy*, 287.

"Calamity Jack," "No. 1 liar": Cash, *Who the Hell Is William Loeb?*, xvii.

"military dictator": McWhorter, Diane, *Carry Me Home*, Simon & Schuster, 2001, 448.

"compromiser with evil": Rowan, Carl, "How Kennedy's concern for Negroes led to his death," *Ebony*, Apr. 1967, 27–34.

"cactus bouquet": Leuchtenburg, *The American President*, 402.

"traitor": Marrs, Jim, *Crossfire: The Plot That Killed Kennedy*, Basic Books, 2013, 7.

"treason handbill": Onion, Rebecca, "The 'Wanted for Treason' flyer distributed in Dallas before JFK's visit," Slate.com, Nov. 15, 2013.

"more wicked than Hitler": Horowitz, David, *Radical Son: A Generational Odyssey*, Simon & Schuster, 2011, 130.

Lyndon B. Johnson (1908–1973; in Office 1963–1969)

"goddam traitor": Mellen, Joan, *Faustian Bargains: Lyndon Johnson and Mac Wallace in the Robber-Baron Culture of Texas*, Bloomsbury, 2016, 138.

"southern Benedict Arnold," "Texas Yankee," "political polygamist": Nelson, Phillip, *LBJ: The Mastermind of the JFK Assassination*, Skyhorse Publishing, 2013, 56.

"Judas candidate," "LBJ sold out to Yankee Socialists": Unger and Unger, *LBJ: A Life*, 251.

"son-of-a-bitch," "wasn't very pleasant," "mean," "abusive," "unstable": Newfield, Jack, *RFK: A Memoir*, Public Affairs, 2009, 131–132.

"Lyndon Benedict Johnson": "Mr. Boston Beans," *NYT*, Sept. 11, 1960.

"faker," "phoniest": *Alabama Journal*, July 15, 1964.

"scheming wire puller": Johnson, Robert David, *All the Way with LBJ: The 1964 Presidential Election*, Cambridge UP, 2009, 224.

"Whitewash House": *Time*, Sept. 25, 1964.

"interim President," "lie-filled": *Burlington Free Press*, Oct. 2, 1964.

"raving, ranting": *NYT*, Sept. 23, 1964.

"mad wild dog," "white honky," "outlaw": Unger and Unger, *LBJ: A Life*, 425.

"rattlesnake," "great hatred": Leuchtenburg, William, *The White House Looks South: Franklin D. Roosevelt, Harry S. Truman, Lyndon B. Johnson*, Louisiana State UP, 2005, 372.

"centaur": Isaacson, and Thomas, *The Wise Men*, 708.

"bully with an Air force," "close to insanity": Lennon, J. Michael, *Norman Mailer*, Simon & Schuster, 2013, 355.

"der Fuehrer": Isaacson and Thomas, *The Wise Men*, 663.

"Dr. Cornpone": Felzenberg, Alvin, *A Man and His Presidents: The Political Odyssey of William F. Buckley Jr.*, Yale UP, 2017, 156.

"big fool": Bianculli, David, *Dangerously Funny: The Uncensored Story of "The Smothers Brothers Comedy Hour,"* Simon & Schuster, 2009, 170.

"'Get those bastards off my back'": 'The Smothers Brothers Comedy Hour' at 50,' *Hollywood Reporter*, Nov. 25, 2017.

"Bullshit Johnson," "biggest liar": Caro, Robert, *The Years of Lyndon Johnson: Means of Ascent*, Knopf, 1990, 50.

"bastard": Solberg, Carl, *Hubert Humphrey: A Biography*, Minnesota Historical Society Press, 2003, 392.

Richard M. Nixon (1913–1994; in Office 1969–August 9, 1974)

"political paranoid": Genovese, *The Watergate Crisis*, 63.

"demagogue," "fear," "Peewee," "backwash": Black, Conrad, *Richard M. Nixon: A Life in Full*, PublicAffairs, 2008, 153, 163.

"well-oiled drawbridge": Greenberg, *Nixon's Shadow*, 59.

"white-collar McCarthy": Brodie, *Richard Nixon*, 291.

"no-good lying bastard": Gallu, Samuel, *Give 'em Hell Harry*, Viking Press, 1975, 76.

"go to Hell": Brodie, *Richard Nixon*, 422.

"filthy lying son-of-a-bitch": Matthews, *Kennedy & Nixon*, 177.

"two-fisted, four-square liar": Pietrusza, David, *1960: LBJ vs. JFK vs. Nixon: The Epic Campaign That Forged Three Presidencies*, Sterling Publishing Company, 2008, 220.

"traitor": Bothmer, Bernard von, *Framing the Sixties: The Use and Abuse of a Decade from Ronald Reagan to George W. Bush*, University of Massachusetts Press, 2010, 16.

"cheap bastard": Matthews, *Kennedy & Nixon*, 208.

"swine": Greenberg, *Nixon's Shadow*, 343.

"Mad Monk": Genovese, *The Watergate Crisis*, 58.

"meatball mind," "drunken friend," "that madman": Dallek, Robert, "The Kissinger presidency," *Vanity Fair*, Apr. 2, 2007.

"shit": Ambrose, Stephen, *Nixon*, Vol. 3, *Ruin and Recovery, 1973–1990*, Simon & Schuster, 1991, 489.

Gerald Ford (1913–2006; in Office 1974–1977)

"it was essential," "portrayal of me": Ford, Gerald, *Humor and the Presidency*, Arbor House, 1987, 48.

"nice guy": Leuchtenburg, *The American President*, 542.

"so dumb": Reeves, *A Ford, Not a Lincoln*, 25.

"Jerry the Jerk," "Babbling Betty": Cash, *Who the Hell Is William Loeb?*, xvi.

"dumb bastard": "GOP kingmaker apologizes for calling Jerry Ford 'dumb,'" *UPUI Archives*, Feb. 12, 1982.

"fine-looking man": *NYT*, Jan. 6, 2007.

"Eisenhower without": Mieczkowski, Yanek, *Gerald Ford and the Challenges of the 1970s*, UP of Kentucky, 2005, 83.

"Old Bungle Foot," "Mr. Ten Thumbs," "America's Pet Rock," "catastrophically close": Rozell, Mark, *The Press and the Ford Presidency*, University of Michigan Press, 1992, 123.

"slow, unimaginative," "triumph": Reeves, *A Ford, Not a Lincoln*, 18, 26.

"cynical, clumsy": New York *Daily News*, Nov. 25, 1975.

"worse than": *National Journal*, Jan. 5, 2012.

Jimmy Carter (b. 1924; in Office 1977–1981)

"pig in a poke": Perlstein, *The Invisible Bridge*, 500.

"Jimmy Hoover?": *NYT*, Feb. 7, 1979.

"Dr. Jekyll": *Santa Ana Register*, Aug. 28, 1976.

"smiling hypocrite," "liar," "phony," "snake oil," "chameleon": Godbold, E. Stanly, Jr., *Jimmy and Rosalynn Carter: The Georgia Years, 1924–1974*, Oxford UP, 2010, 156.

"dangerous": Perlstein, *The Invisible Bridge*, 500.

"Southern-fried": Lechner, Zachary, *The South of the Mind: American Imaginings of White Southernness, 1960–1980*, University of Georgia Press, 2018, 156.

"Reagan clone": Reinhart, David, *The Republican Right Since 1945*, University of Kentucky Press, 2013, 237.

"worst failure": *Los Angeles Times*, May 31, 1980.

"oratorical mortician": Leuchtenburg, *The American President*, 561.

"Missionary lectern-pounding": Wolfe, Tom, *Mauve Gloves and Madmen, Clutter and Vine*, Macmillan, 1976, 134.

"complete birdbrain": *New York Magazine*, Dec. 21, 1981, 13.

"goddamn liar": *Texas Monthly*, Oct. 1986, 135–137.

"biggest flip-flopper": *Bee* (Danville, Virginia), Aug. 30, 1976.

"little schmuck": Brinkley, Douglas, *The Unfinished Presidency: Jimmy Carter's Journey Beyond the White House*, Penguin, 1998, 14.

"leftist," "stupid": *WaPo*, Sept. 14, 1981.

"waste of skin": *The Glenn Beck Program*, Feb. 8, 2006, Premiere Radio Network.

"disaster": DeFrank and Ford, *Write It When I'm Gone*, 145.

Chapter Seven

Ronald Reagan (1911–2004; in Office 1981–1987)

"Ronald for Real": *Time*, Oct. 7, 1966.

"Teflon-coated President": Schroeder, Patricia, Remarks to the House of Representatives, Aug. 2, 1983.

"extremist," "enemy": *NYT*, Sept. 12, 1966.

"petrified pig": *NYT*, May 22, 1988.

"ignorant," "Hoover with a smile": *NYT*, Jan. 7, 1994.

"brains," "limited": "Ronald Reagan's birth centennial, Part I: Politics came late in his life," *Los Angeles Times*, Feb. 4, 2011.

"dumb": Wills, Garry, "If Reagan's not senile, why does he talk that way," syndicated column, *Lincoln Journal Star*, Apr. 17, 1980.

"economic madness," "voodoo economics": Howison, Jeffrey, *The 1980 Presidential Election: Ronald Reagan and the Shaping of the American Conservative Movement*, Routledge, 2014, 108.

"life seems": Carter, Jimmy, *White House Diary*, Farrar, Strauss and Giroux, 2010, 513.

"nothing between his ears": Pugliese, Stanislao, *The Political Legacy of Margaret Thatcher*, Politico's, 2003, 376.

"useful idiot," "weak man," "speech reader-in-chief": *Los Angeles Times*, Dec. 5, 1987.

"neither fox nor hedgehog": Hitchens, Christopher, "Not even a hedgehog," Slate.com, June 7, 2004.

"triumph of the embalmer's art": Hensher, Philip, "Gore Vidal: the man who knew everyone," *Telegraph*, Aug. 1, 2012.

George H. W. Bush (1924–2018; in Office 1989–1993)

"doesn't seem to stand for anything": *Newsweek*, Mar. 8, 1992.

"the only guy": Brown, Sherrod, *Congress from the Inside: Observations from the Majority and the Minority*, Kent State UP, 2004, 69.

"Wimp Factor": *Newsweek*, Oct. 19, 1987.

"carpetbagger": Corrigan, Matthew, *American Royalty: The Bush and Clinton Families and the Danger to the Presidency*, Springer, 2008, 61.

"born with a silver foot": Transcript of the keynote address at the 1988 Democratic National Convention by Ann Richards, the Texas treasurer, *NYT*, July 19, 1988.

"pin-stripin' polo-playin'": "The Republicans in '88," *Atlantic*, July 1987.

"I'll get you some day," "play by the rules": "Fast times at Nashua High," *National Review*, Oct. 19, 2009.

"man who freezes": Frankel, Benjamin, *The Cold War: 1945–1991*, Gale, 1992, 78.

"placed his manhood": Bates, Eric, "The *Rolling Stone* interview: Garry Trudeau," *Rolling Stone*, Aug. 5, 2004.

"silly and effeminate": Stahl, Lesley, *Reporting Live*, Simon & Schuster, 1999, 313.

"eunuch": Curtis, Bruce, "The wimp factor," *American Heritage*, Nov. 1989.

"King George": *WaPo*, Feb. 23, 1992.

"Pekingese": Will, George, "And a Germany 'As mutable as the sea,'" *Baltimore Sun*, Dec. 14, 1989.

"lapdog": *WaPo*, Sept. 26, 1986.

"lighter than air": Will, George, "Flippant style, trivial pursuits," *Newsweek*, Nov. 4, 1990.

"running for First Lady": *NYT*, Aug. 20, 1992.

Bill Clinton (b. 1946; in Office 1993–2001)

"Slick Willy," "Kid Clinton," "Boy Governor," "young Smoothie": "It's come to this: A nickname that's proven hard to slip," *WaPo*, Dec. 20, 1998.

"discomfiting tendency": "Bill Clinton's promise," *NYT*, Oct. 22, 1992.

The Clinton Chronicles: Matrisciana, Patrick, *The Clinton Chronicles*, Jeremiah Films, 1994.

"Communication Stream": "White House memo asserts a scandal theory," *WaPo*, Jan. 10, 1997.

"did inhale": Hutchison, Kay Bailey, Address to the Republican National Convention, Houston, Aug. 17, 1992.

"nerdy": *LA Times*, Oct. 11, 1992.

"draft-dodging": Buchanan, Patrick, Address to the Republican National Convention, Houston, Aug. 17, 1992.

"bozos": Bush campaign speech in Michigan, Oct. 29, 1992.

"Waffle Man": Bush campaign speech in Stevens Point, Wisconsin, Oct. 31, 1992.

"dodging the draft," "slippery when wet": *NYT*, Sept. 23, 1992.

"Communist": Brock, David, *Blinded by the Right*, Three Rivers Press, 2003, 139.

"spoiled brat," "gone to hell": "New memoirs quote Nixon on Clintons," United Press International Archives, July 21, 1996, upi.com.

"enemy of normal Americans": "Abroad at Home: Eye of Newt," *NYT*, Nov. 14, 1994.

Gingrich memo: "Language: A key mechanism of control." In A. D. Bernstein and P. W. Bernstein, eds., *Quotations from Speaker Newt: The Little Red, White, and Blue Book of the Republican Revolution*, Workman Publishing, 1995.

"bore": "Brinkley's parting shots at Clinton," *WaPo*, Nov. 7, 1996.

"big creep": "The 'Monica show,'" *Chicago Tribune*, Aug. 6, 1998.

"slut": "Candidate calls Clinton 'slut,'" *SFGate.com*, Apr. 8, 1998.

"scumbag": *Chicago Tribune*, Sept. 13, 1998.

"President Caligula": "The President under fire," *NYT*, Jan. 31, 1998.

"murderer": *The View*, ABC, Nov. 16, 2000.

"predator": *Esquire*, Aug. 30, 2016.

George W. Bush (b. 1946; in Office 2001–2009)

"misunderestimated," "food on your family": Weisberg, Jacob, *The Deluxe Election-Edition Bushisms: The First Term, in His Own Special Words*, Simon & Schuster, 2004.

"playground bully": Wolff, Michael, "This media life: Saint George," *New York Magazine*, Dec. 10, 2001.

"only guy in history": *NYT*, Dec. 9, 2001.

"I've been": *Public Papers of the Presidents of the United States: George W. Bush, Administration of George W. Bush*, Mar. 7, 2007, 257.

"lot of criticism," "Conway West": "Kanye West apologises for calling George Bush a racist," *Guardian*, Nov. 10, 2010.

"Shrub": Ivins and Dubose, *Shrub*. Ivins is credited with coining the nickname.

"frat-boy": *WaPo*, Aug. 12, 1999.

"dyslexic": Hitchens, "Why Dubya can't read."

"empty suit": Kakutani, Michiko, "Presidential confidential: Bill Clinton after hours," *NYT*, Sept. 24, 2009.

"fake cowboy": "George W. Bush ain't no cowboy," *Village Voice*, Sept. 28, 2004.

"chest beater": Faludi, Susan, *The Terror Dream: Fear and Fantasy in Post-9/11 America*, Holt, 2007, 3.

"monkey": *Morning Joe*, MSNBC, Nov. 26, 2007.

"feckless": Kushner, Tony, "Afterword," to *Homebody/Kabul: Revised Version*, Theatre Communications Group, 2004, 189.

"treacherous little freak": Sullivan, James, "Hunter S. Thompson dies," *Rolling Stone*, Feb. 21, 2005.

"high-functioning moron": *Anderson Cooper 360 Degrees*, CNN.com, Sept. 25, 2008.

"chicken hawk": Crowley, Michael, "Paul Hackett's near-victory," *New Republic*, Aug. 14, 2005.

"deserter": Lang, Thomas, "Peter Jennings vs. Wesley Clark vs. Michael Moore vs. George W. Bush," *Columbia Journalism Review*, Jan. 26, 2004.

"loser": "The eight craziest stories about Harry Reid," *Atlantic*, Mar. 27, 2015.

Barack Obama (b. 1961; in Office 2009–2017)

"has yet to have to prove": "Anti-Obama 'birther movement' gathers steam," Guardian.com, July 28, 2009.

"Now you know": "GOP official defends Obama chimpanzee email," *L.A. NOW*, LATimes.com, Apr. 17, 2011.

"Kenyan, anti-colonial": "Gingrich, D'Souza, 'Kenyan anti-colonialism' and the mainstream-kook convergence," *New Republic*, Sept. 13, 2010.

"affirmative action candidate": Chafets, Zev, "Late-period Limbaugh," *NYT Magazine*, July 6, 2008.

"food stamp president": "Barack Obama: The 'food-stamp president'?," *WaPo*, Dec. 8, 2011.

"racist": "Fox News commentator calls Barack Obama racist," Telegraph.com, July 29, 2009.

"acting like": "Jackson slams Obama for 'acting white,'" Politico.com, Sept. 19, 2007.

"anti-Christ": "Obama heckled as 'Antichrist' at Hollywood fundraiser," Businessinsider.com, Sept. 27, 2011.

"would pay": "Meghan McCain: Obama 'a dirty capitalist like the rest of us,'" Hill.com, Apr. 4, 2017.

"snob": "Santorum presses culture wars attack," *WaPo*, Feb. 26, 2012.

"Chicago political machine": "The ad campaign: Obama's Chicago, in McCain's eyes," *NYT*, Sept. 22, 2008.

"unhinged": "Think Fox's anti-Obama ad was bad? Here are ten worse things they've said," Rollingstone.com, June 1, 2012.

"wuss": *Tucker*, MSNBC, July 2, 2007.

"pussy": "Fox business guest explodes," *Huffington Post*, Dec. 7, 2015.

"food stamp president": "Gingrich promises to slash taxes, calls Obama 'food stamp president,'" *WaPo*, May 13, 2011.

"Kenyan creampuff": "#StayWoke: Take a look at Trump's Energy appointee's deleted Tweets about Blacks, Jews and women," Root.com, June 23, 2017.

"stupid": "Palin: Obama 'is a special kind of stupid,'" Politico.com, June 17, 2016.

"weak-kneed": "Sarah Palin's rambling, remarkable and at times hard to understand endorsement of Donald Trump," *WaPo*, Jan. 20, 2016.

"puppet": Lowkey, *Obama Nation Part 2* (featuring Black the Ripper and M-1), Mesopotamia Music, 2011.

"lazy": "Sununu calls Obama lazy, disengaged and incompetent," Politico.com, Oct. 4, 2012.

"dirty capitalist": Megan McCain, "Outnumbered," *Fox News*, Apr. 27, 2017.

"deporter-in-chief": "Obama vs. Trump: Who has deported more immigrants?," *Newsweek*, Apr. 18, 2017.

"moron": "Giuliani on Obama's Iran negotiations," Real Clear Politics.com, Feb. 22, 2015.

"founder": "Donald Trump calls Obama 'founder of ISIS' and says it honors him," *NYT*, Aug. 10, 2016.

"dictator": "Maine Gov. Paul LePage: Barack Obama is a dictator," CNN.com, Oct. 12, 2016.

"dick": "MSNBC suspends analyst Halperin for Obama remark," Reuters.com, June 30, 2011.

Trump (b. 1942; in Office 2017–)
"Mr. Meltdown": Donald Trump (@realDonaldTrump), Twitter, Feb. 26, 2016.

SOURCES AND BIBLIOGRAPHY

"Lyin' Ted": Donald Trump (@realDonaldTrump), Twitter, Apr. 26, 2016.

"sad sack," "spoiled child," "lightweight," "puppet": Lee, Jasmine C., and Kevin Quealy, "The 567 people, places and things Donald Trump has insulted on Twitter: A complete list," New York Times.com, Feb. 20, 2019.

"Look at that face!": Solotaroff, Paul, "Trump seriously: On the trail with the GOP's tough guy," *Rolling Stone*, Sept. 9, 2015.

"Hillary Clinton is a liar": *60 Minutes*, July 17, 2016.

"Crooked Hillary," "Lock her up": "At Florida rally, Trump resumes attacking 'Crooked Hillary Clinton,'" *WaPo*, Sept. 27, 2016.

"She doesn't have the look": Transcript of the first Clinton-Trump debate, New York Times.com, Sept. 27, 2016.

"tremendous hate," "be in jail," "devil": Transcript of the second Clinton-Trump debate," New York Times.com, Oct. 10, 2016.

"have a puppet," "You're the puppet!," "Such a nasty woman": Transcript of the third Clinton-Trump debate, New York Times.com, Oct. 20, 2016.

"weak," "dumb," "crazy," "enemies": Lee and Quealy, "The 567 people, places and things."

"short-fingered vulgarian": "Trump nemesis Graydon Carter is leaving Vanity Fair," *WaPo*, Sept. 7, 2017.

"orange prince": "61 not-very-positive things foreign leaders have said about Donald Trump," *WaPo*, May 6, 2016.

"President Cheeto": https://twitter.com/PresidentCheeto, among others.

"motherfucker": "Rashida Tlaib's expletive-laden cry to impeach Trump upends Democrats' talking points," New York Times.com, Jan. 4, 2019.

"thirteen-year-old": "8 times Chris Christie suggested Donald Trump shouldn't be president," Politico.com, Feb. 26, 2016.

"sniveling coward": "Ted Cruz warns Donald Trump to leave his wife 'the hell alone,'" New York Times.com, Mar. 24, 2016.

"big, loud": "14 times Donald Trump and Ted Cruz insulted each other," Time.com, Sept. 23, 2016.

"phony," "con artist": "Mitt Romney calls Donald Trump 'a phony, a fraud': Trump hits back," NPR.org, Mar. 3, 2016.

"jackass," "kook," "bigot": Miller, Lisa, "The little jerk," *New York Magazine*, Sept. 16, 2018.

"malignant clown": Mark Kirk (@SenatorKirk), Twitter, Oct. 7, 2016.

"jagoff": Morin, Rebecca, "Endorsing Clinton, Mark Cuban calls Trump a 'jagoff,'" Politico.com, July 30, 2016.

"fascist, loofa-faced shit-gibbon": Daylin Leach (@daylinleach), Twitter, Feb. 7, 2017.

"unhinged": Reich, Robert, "Introducing Donald Trump, the biggest loser," Newsweek.com, July 31, 2017.

"asshole": "Rep. Duncan Hunter gives President Trump a profane compliment," *Los Angeles Times*, Aug. 28, 2017.

"fucking moron": Filkins, Dexter, "Rex Tillerson at the breaking point," *New Yorker*, Oct. 16, 2017.

"Woody Allen," "weak and sniveling," "drama queen": Noonan, Peggy, "Trump Is Woody Allen without the humor," WSJ.com, July 27, 2017.

"Lazy Boy," "bored and tired": "Trump, America's boy king," *Newsweek*, Aug. 1, 2017.

"President Spanky": *The Late Show with Stephen Colbert*, CBS, Mar. 27, 2018.

"economic traitor": Kotlikoff, Laurence, "Time to call Trump by his real name—economic traitor," Forbes.com, July 12, 2018.

"traitor": Blow, Charles, "Trump, treasonous traitor," *NYT*, July 15, 2018.

"little wet noodle": "Schwarzenegger calls Trump a 'little wet noodle' and a 'fanboy' after Putin news conference," *Los Angeles Times*, July 17, 2018.

"biggest wimp": Ann Coulter (@AnnCoulter), Twitter, Jan. 24, 2019.

Sidebars

"Fake News?": *United States v. Hudson*, 11 U.S. 32 (1812); Roosevelt, Theodore, Special Message to the Two Houses of Congress, December 15, 1908; *United States v. Press Publishing Co.*, 219 U.S. 1 (1911); Beito, David, "FDR's War Against the Press,"Reason.com, May 2017, New York *Times Co. v. Sullivan*, 376 U.S. 254 (1964).

"pusillanimous," "pussy," "dotard," "superannuated," "doughface," "copperhead," "flathead," "fathead," "idiot," "imbecile," "moron," "yellow," "bloviate," "socialist," "jerk," "asshole," "ass," "jackass," "wimp": *OED Online*, July 2018, Oxford UP.

"timid pussyfooters": *Freeport (IL) Journal-Standard*, Sept. 21, 1940.

"pussyfooting and dodging": *Fort Myers News-Press*, Oct. 19, 1960.

"doughface": Bartlett, John Russell, *Dictionary of Americanisms*, Little Brown, 1884; Stimpson, George W., *A Book about American Politics*, Harper, 1952, 35. Stimpson notes that the phrase "a Northern man with Southern principles" was first used to refer to Martin Van Buren.

"Stop the Presses": Tebbel and Watts, *The Press and the Presidency*, 191–196; Winfield, Betty Houchin, *FDR and the News Media*, Columbia UP, 1994, 173–179.

"yellow": "Is this the great yellow race," *Chicago Tribune*, Oct. 20, 2016, 8.

SOURCES AND BIBLIOGRAPHY

"asshole": Nunberg, Geoffrey, *Ascent of the A-Word: Assholism, the First Sixty Years*, Public Affairs, 2012.

"bloviate": Brokaw, Clare Boothe, "Men must bloviate," *Pittsburgh Post-Gazette*, Sept. 28, 1934, 24.

"socialist": Varney, Harold Lloyd, *Chicago Tribune*, Oct. 1 and 2, 1936; Brown, George Rothwell, "The Political parade," *San Francisco Examiner*, Oct. 6, 1949; Pegler, Westbrook, "Fair Enough," syndicated column, *Clovis (NM) News Journal*, July 25, 1952; "GOP group raps Nixon, Reagan," *Oakland Tribune*, Feb 21. 1971; Goldberg, Michelle, "The millennial socialists are coming," *NYT*, June 30, 2018; Gstalter, Morgan, "Democratic Socialists of America see membership spike after Ocasio-Cortez win," thehill.com, June 28, 2018; Newport, Frank, "The meaning of 'socialism' to Americans today," Polling Matters, Gallup.com, Oct. 4, 2018.

"jerk": Lighter, Jonathan, *Random House Historical Dictionary of American Slang*, Vol. 2, H-O, Random House, 1997; Turner, Timothy G., "Jerry the Jerk speaks of Mayor Beethoven," *Los Angeles Times*, Sept. 20, 1943, 19; "Is this a Ford we should buy?," *Manchester Union Leader*, May 31, 1974.

"wimp": Poston, Lawrence, "Some problems in the study of campus slang," *American Speech* 39, no. 2 (1964): 114–123; Poston, Lawrence, and Francis J. Stillman, "Notes on campus vocabulary, 1964," *American Speech* 40, no. 3 (1965): 193–195; McAtee, W. T., untitled, *The Railway Conductor* (1919): 377–380.

Bibliography

Adams, John Quincy. *Memoirs of John Quincy Adams*. Lippincott, 1877.

Baker, Jean. *James Buchanan*. Macmillan, 2004.

Benton, T. H. *Abridgment of the Debates of Congress, from 1789 to 1856: April 15, 1824–March 10, 1826*, D. Appleton, 1860.

Black, Andrew. *John Pendleton Kennedy: Early American Novelist, Whig Statesman, and Ardent Nationalist*. Louisiana State UP, 2016.

Boller, Paul. *Not So! Popular Myths About America from Columbus to Clinton*. Oxford UP, 1995.

Boller, Paul. *Presidential Anecdotes*. Oxford UP, 1996.

Boller, Paul. *Presidential Campaigns: From George Washington to George W. Bush*. Oxford UP, 2004.

Brinkley, Alan, and Davis Dyer, eds. *The American Presidency*, Houghton Mifflin, 2004.

Brodie, Fawn M. *Richard Nixon: The Shaping of His Character*, Harvard UP, 1983.

Burstein, Andrew, and Nancy Isenberg. *Madison and Jefferson*. Random House, 2010.

Byrnes, Mark. *James K. Polk: A Biographical Companion*. ABC-CLIO, 2001.

Callendar, James. *The Prospect Before Us*. Jones, Pleasants and Field, 1800.

Cash, Kevin. *Who the Hell Is William Loeb?* Amoskeag Press, 1975.

Chace, James. *1912: Wilson, Roosevelt, Taft & Debs; The Election That Changed the Country*, Simon & Schuster, 2004.

Chernow, Ron. *Alexander Hamilton*. Penguin, 2004.

Chernow, Ron. *Grant*. Penguin, 2017.

Chernow, Ron. *Washington: A Life*. Penguin, 2010.

Coletta, Paolo. *The Presidency of William Howard Taft*. UP of Kansas, 1973.

Collins, Gail. *William Henry Harrison*. Macmillan, 2012.

Crapol, Edward. *John Tyler, the Accidental President*. University of North Carolina Press, 2012.

Dean, John W., and Robertson Dean. *Warren G. Harding*. Macmillan, 2004.

DeFrank, Thomas, and Gerald Ford. *Write It When I'm Gone: Remarkable Off-the-Record Conversations with Gerald R. Ford*. Penguin, 2007.

Flynt, Larry, and David Eisenbach. *One Nation Under Sex: How the Private Lives of Presidents, First Ladies and Their Lovers Changed the Course of American History*. St. Martin's, 2011.

Gardner, Gerald. *Campaign Comedy: Political Humor from Clinton to Kennedy*. Wayne State UP, 1994.

Genovese, Michael. *The Watergate Crisis*. Greenwood, 1999.

Greenberg, David. *Nixon's Shadow: The History of an Image*. Norton, 2004.

Hamilton, Holman. *Zachary Taylor: Soldier in the White House*. Bobbs-Merrill, 1941.

Han, Lori Cox, ed. *Hatred of America's Presidents: Personal Attacks on the White House from Washington to Trump*. ABC-CLIO, 2018.

Holt, Michael. *Franklin Pierce*. Macmillan, 2010.

Holt, Michael. *The Rise and Fall of the American Whig Party*. Oxford UP, 2003.

Hutchins, Stilson. *The 1880 Democratic Campaign Handbook*. Democratic National Committee, 1880.

Isaacson, Walter, and Evan Thomas. *The Wise Men: Six Friends and the World They Made*. Simon & Schuster, 2012.

Ivins, Molly, and Lou Dubose. *Shrub: The Short but Happy Political Life of George W. Bush*. Random House, 2000.

Kinzer, Stephen. *The True Flag: Theodore Roosevelt, Mark Twain, and the Birth of American Empire*. Holt, 2017.

Klein, Philip. *President James Buchanan, a Biography.* Pennsylvania State UP, 1962.

Leuchtenburg, William. *The American President: From Teddy Roosevelt to Bill Clinton.* Oxford UP, 2015.

Leuchtenburg, William. *The FDR Years: On Roosevelt and His Legacy.* Columbia UP, 1997.

Leuchtenburg, William. *In the Shadow of FDR: From Harry Truman to George W. Bush.* Cornell UP, 2001.

Longworth, Alice R. *Crowded Hours.* Charles Scribner's Sons, 1933.

Matthews, Chris. *Kennedy & Nixon: The Rivalry That Shaped Postwar America,* Simon & Schuster, 2011.

May, Gary. *John Tyler.* Macmillan, 2008.

McCullough, David. *John Adams.* Simon & Schuster, 2002.

McCullough, David. *Truman.* Simon & Schuster, 2003.

Mencken, H. L. *On Politics: A Carnival of Buncombe.* Johns Hopkins UP, 1956.

Miller, Merle. *Plain Speaking.* G. P. Putnam's Sons, 1974.

Monroe, R. Daniel. *The Republican Vision of John Tyler.* Texas A&M UP, 2003.

Nowlan, Robert. *The American Presidents, from Polk to Hayes: What They Did, What They Said, What Was Said About Them, with Full Source Notes.* Outskirts Press, 2016.

Nowlan, Robert. *The American Presidents, from Washington to Tyler: What They Did, What They Said, What Was Said About Them, with Full Source Notes.* McFarland, 2012.

Perlstein, Rick. *The Invisible Bridge: The Fall of Nixon and the Rise of Reagan.* Simon & Schuster, 2015.

Peskin, Allan, *Garfield: A Biography.* Kent State UP, 1978.

Polk, James K. *The Diary of a President: 1845–1849.* Longmans, Green and Co., 1952.

Reeves, Richard. *A Ford, Not a Lincoln,* Harcourt Brace, 1975.

Remini, Robert V. *Andrew Jackson: The Course of American Freedom, 1822–1832.* Vol. 2. Johns Hopkins UP, 2013.

Remini, Robert V. *John Quincy Adams.* Macmillan, 2002.

Scharnhorst, Gary, *Julian Hawthorne: The Life of a Prodigal Son.* University of Illinois Press, 2014.

Sheppard, Si. *The Partisan Press: A History of Media Bias in the United States.* McFarland, 2007.

Spragens, William C., ed. *Popular Images of American Presidents.* Greenwood Publishing Group, 1988.

Tagg, James. *Benjamin Franklin Bache and the Philadelphia Aurora*. University of Pennsylvania Press, 1991.

Tagg, Larry. *The Unpopular Mr. Lincoln*. Savas Beattie, 2009.

Tebbel, John William, and Sarah Miles Watts. *The Press and the Presidency: From George Washington to Ronald Reagan*. Oxford UP, 1985.

Unger, Irwin, and Debi Unger. *LBJ: A Life*. Wiley, 1999.

Welch, Richard. *The Presidencies of Grover Cleveland*. UP of Kansas, 1988.

Whitcomb, John, and Claire Whitcomb. *Real Life at the White House: Two Hundred Years of Daily Life at America's Most Famous Residence*. Psychology Press, 2002.

Widmer, Ted. *Martin Van Buren*. Macmillan, 2005.

Index

For the benefit of digital users, indexed terms that span two pages (e.g., 52–53) may, on occasion, appear on only one of those pages.